"Many of us have given much of our lives to build, renew, and understand the mystery of faith community. I only wish we would have had the Whiteheads' book twenty years ago! Again they bring intelligence, maturity, and often brilliant counsel to the enduring human task: How do we live together as sisters and brothers?"

Richard Rohr, O.F.M.
Albuquerque, N.M.

"As we have come to expect from the authors, *Community of Faith* delivers what it promises! This very comprehensive book brings together the social sciences, the Christian tradition, and the lived experience of a great variety of communities. Having explored the biblical call to community, they look, skillfully and re-alistically, at expectations, behaviors, skills, leadership, hopes and dreams."

Mary Bennet McKinney, O.S.B., D.Min.

"The Whiteheads have again provided an unparalleled service to those who are crafting contexts of interdependence of in-dividuals within groups and communities. *Community of Faith* faces this challenge wholistically by using models of theology, sociology, and psychology. The authors develop the idea that an authentic Christian anthropology and sociology is rooted in tra-ditional metaphors such as vocation and the Kingdom of God. Consequently, they give to those of us in academia and pastoral ministry a new hope and awareness for our mission."

Elaine Scully, R.S.M.
Providence College

"If you have not read the original version of this book, then you are in for a treat, especially in its theoretical and practical im-plications for small faith communities. If you have read the first edition of *Community of Faith*, read it again in this revision. You will find many new treasures....It reshapes the best of the orig-inal edition to fit the recent attention given to small communities; it adds new insights and resources for those interested in making communities, of any type, more effective."

Thomas Sweetser, S.J.
Co-Director, Parish Evaluation Project

"*Community of Faith* is a clear and concise resource for leadership working to build communities of faith in our church as well as for the communities themselves. It is a 'how, what, and why' for the most significant ecclesiastical development of our times. Evelyn Eaton, Jim Whitehead, and Michael Cowan are authentic and instructive witnesses to a new style of being church!"

Rosemary Bleuher
Chair: North American Forum for Small Christian Communities

"At Communitas we welcome *Community of Faith* for the questions and complexities it raises. It challenges us in our reality and our own ambiguities. We say of ourselves that we embrace the creative tensions of a rich tradition from the past, an ever-changing present, and an uncertain future. This book is what we need at this point in our community life that spans twenty years and many changes."

Maureen Healy
Pastoral Minister, Communitas

"The new *Communities of Faith* is not a 'mere' revision, but a serious rewriting that reflects ten additional years (since the original publication) of serious experimentation with small Christian communities in the U.S. church. It is precisely because the Whiteheads are such good 'on-their-feet' theologians that a decade of new experience requires of them *new* theological reflection.

"Forming a small Christian community is not easy. Careful discussion of this book, chapter by chapter, won't solve a community's problems, but will help it to get some common language for processing its life, and provide ample materials from theology and the social sciences to frame its challenges."

Bernard J. Lee, S.M.
Loyola University, New Orleans

"This book is for all of us who search for community but find its meaning elusive. The Whiteheads stimulate our imaginations to dream of community in new ways and with new possibilities and offer us 'tools' for crafting an environment in which community formation may grow. As always, they communicate a vision of both/and possibilities for our ongoing process of life development which is encouraging, supportive, and inclusive."

Sharon Casey, O.P.
Dominican School of Philosophy and Theology

Foreword by Rev. Arthur Baranowski

COMMUNITY of faith

Crafting Christian Communities Today

EVELYN EATON WHITEHEAD
JAMES D. WHITEHEAD

TWENTY-THIRD PUBLICATIONS

Mystic, Connecticut 06355

Books by the Whiteheads

Community of Faith
Christian Life Patterns
The Promise of Partnership
A Sense of Sexuality
The Emerging Laity
Seasons of Strength
Marrying Well
Method in Ministry

Twenty-Third Publications
185 Willow Street
P.O. Box 180
Mystic CT 06355
(203) 536-2611
800-321-0411

ISBN 0-89622-518-6
Library of Congress Catalog Card Number 92-81799

Foreword

"Community" and "mission" are high-sounding rhetoric for most people, the stuff of sermons. Real life is taken up with surviving family crises, managing job changes, and finding energy to keep up the home and funds to pay the taxes. For millions of new immigrants among us, for most of whom English is a second language, concerns of sheer survival dominate. And, of course, these days nobody has enough time!

For the person in the pew—and for those who have stopped filling the pew—small church communities make a connection between everyday life and faith possible. Work, family life, and civic involvement become places where God can be found. The people in these small communities may never quite get comfortable with the language of community and mission but they experience what these terms try to name.

In the West and certainly in the United States, religion may be important but religion is seen as private and individual. Beliefs are meant to influence one's personal life and decisions, not the corporate life of the nation or its existing institutions. So when religious leaders speak on issues of the economy or armaments, they are politely dismissed as out of their field of competence. Their "field" is the private lives of their flocks. But often even here, religion makes little difference. A new study program or another pastoral letter just do not get through to people's experience. How are the majority of the thousands of Christians in our country to make connections between life and faith unless they begin to share life with other believers in some regular way?

The power of this kind of faith group has to be experienced to be believed. The faith community creates an environment that helps people be different. Small faith groups can change people's lives and help them maintain that transformation. Today, this experience of small groups is widespread: twelve-step recovery programs, quality work circles, support groups for those suffering the loss of a loved one or the termination of a job. Small groups work!

Isn't Christianity in the business of behavioral change? Isn't the church about giving people an alternative vision to that offered by their culture? Americans today are bombarded by facts and words. This information glut is constant and makes it difficult for people to see what really counts in life or how daily events are connected in any meaningful pattern. As a people, Americans are very private: even in families there is often little sense of what others here are facing or feeling. And, of course, people move so much more often than previously. On top of all this, everyday living is so fast-paced. The result of these trends is a non-reflective society. People live without noticing what happens from day to day or how they are affected. Noticing and valuing the ordinary events of one's life—this basic value must be regained for people to live lives that are richly human and Christian.

Small communities recapture this missing ingredient. In these groups people learn to slow down, to take time, to listen to themselves and other people. This makes faith communities counter-cultural. The small community values the life experience of each person; people begin to recognize that their lives are sacred. What one earns or owns becomes less significant; who one is and how one sees life become more important. The process is gradual, but gathering regularly as a community offers reinforcement in an alternative way of life.

The small church community makes people different. People who might seem unlikely candidates—the harried executive, the traveling salesperson, the affluent retired couple, the shy member at the margins of the parish, the angry advocate of a social cause—change under the influence of this simple process of shared reflection. The exact moment of conversion often cannot be documented, but the change is real.

When the small community is an ongoing part of their experience, people come to appreciate their life more deeply. They go further, asking how God might be speaking to them in these daily events. In faith communities, the question of God's action in our lives keeps getting raised, even if we are not always immediately clear about the answers. Quite ordinary people start to believe in the life they have and to look for God to be part of their own everyday world. In small faith communities, emphasis is on people's lived experience, seen through the lens of Scripture and their religious tradition. This basic religious identity is no longer just for Sunday; it touches all of their life.

Small communities of faith strengthen family and parish life. Today family includes much more than the traditional image of two parents and their children living in the same home. Contemporary families come in many different shapes. Whatever its particular shape, whatever its strengths and wounds, the family is the most basic church. At present, this "domestic church" has few effective connections with the typical large parish. The network of small faith communities provides an intermediate level of church, smaller and more intimate than the usual parish congregations.

How might this small church community affect the family? First, as individuals grow in valuing everyday life and making faith connections, they take that awareness back to their households. Second, if the small community teaches anything it is the simple discipline of listening well. That skill is carried back to the home as well. Spouses learn to speak to each other about their personal hopes and concerns as they learn to bring these issues to the faith group. And both parents and children learn to speak of and listen to the dreams and failures of their lives, and to look for God who is there in all of this.

As a pastor, I have seen the positive effects of small communities on parish life. The most significant change is that community members start to speak of the church as "we" instead of "they." My many homilies on this theme never seemed to make much difference on parishioners' consciousness. But the experience of *belonging*—really sharing life with ten or so fellow believers over a few years—led parishioners to *believe* they are the people of God. And they recognized they belong to the church not because they were contributing money or serving as volunteers (that's what culture is telling them all the time!). Our people came to know that they belong because of *who they are*. They came to recognize that their experience of life and faith (and even lack of faith) is *needed* by the church.

In my experience, *time* was the greatest obstacle we faced in developing small faith communities in our parish. Inviting people—many of whom felt they were already overextended—to consider sharing time with their neighbors in faith reflection was our first step. This required us to keep parish programming to a minimum so that parishioners received a clear message of the priority of these small faith communities.

Rather than add small communities as one more activity, many congregations today are working to make faith communities the basic structure of the parish. These small faith groups gradually develop the characteristics basic to the experience of church: a sense of belonging, shared prayer, faith formation, leadership responsibilities, and a commitment to ministry and service that emerges from this shared life. Through the National Alliance of Parishes Restructuring into Communities (NAPRC), my own active commitment to the vision of small communities of faith continues.

I am pleased to contribute these convictions from my own experience as the foreword to *Community of Faith*. Having used the original edition in my own ministry of community formation, I am delighted that Evelyn and Jim are making their perspective available again in this revised and expanded form. Their work is both visionary and practical. They serve well the new church taking shape in small communities of faith in this country and worldwide.

Rev. Arthur Baranowski
Director, NAPRC

Preface

We are grateful to the many colleagues who encouraged us to prepare this new edition of *Community of Faith* and return it to press. Our thanks go first to Gerard V. Egan and J. Gordon Myers, colleagues at the Institute of Pastoral Studies at Loyola University of Chicago, within whose creative ambience our perspective on community initially developed. By their interest and critique, Joan Scanlon, Lucien Roy, William Thompson, and James Zullo encouraged us to bring the material to print initially. For their support of the revision process, we thank especially Jean Bohr, Linda Lapiers, Bernard Lee, Elaine Scully, Terry Veling, and David Turner.

In our revision, the original manuscript has been completely reworked to incorporate theoretical and practical developments in small groups over the past decade. Dee Ready assisted us here, as she has elsewhere, to simplify our writing style as we prepared new drafts of each chapter. We have updated the listing of resources included in each chapter, adding valuable references that have appeared recently. The flow of the chapters has been redesigned to connect the theological discussion more immediately with the sociological and psychological analysis. Working exercises end each chapter, helping readers apply the analysis to their own setting. When these reflective exercises are shared among members of a faith community, the chapters serve as a practical tool of community formation.

Two new chapters have been added: Chapter Ten on the role of the leader, and Chapter Eleven, provided by Professor Michael Cowan of the Institute for Ministry at Loyola University in New Orleans, charting the development of a small intentional community or "house church." We are especially grateful to Mike, friend and colleague, for letting us include this new material from his ongoing analysis of community life, as well as his discussion of mutuality from our first edition, which appears now in Chapter Thirteen.

For
Mary and Gene Ulrich
Sabrina, Ivan, Megan, Laura
where community begins

CONTENTS

PART ONE
FORMING THE COMMUNITY OF FAITH

PART TWO
SEEKING TOGETHER THE KINGDOM OF GOD

PART THREE
PARTICIPATING IN THE COMMUNITY OF FAITH

COMMUNITY
of faith

INTRODUCTION

Christianity is a community event. The followers of Jesus have always believed that faith is a communal venture, not a private enterprise. Christians today, knowing ourselves to be the people of God, long to experience our life together as community. But many of us sense that this goal is both a gift and a difficult ambition.

The language of church life is often filled with the vocabulary of mutuality: faith sharing, mutual support, communal decision making, partnership, and collaboration. These ideals generate renewed commitment to the ministry of developing community. But for some of us, these ideals have become stumbling blocks. Having given ourselves generously to the effort of community formation, we come away with a sense of frustration and failure. Team ministry is more difficult that we imagined it would be; parish councils have not lived up to early expectations; faith-sharing groups seem so short-lived; shared decision making has been, in practice, a rare phenomenon. Confronted with this gap between our religious rhetoric and our actual experience, we are forced to reexamine our expectations of Christian community.

In the chapters that follow we take up this effort of reexamination. The discussion of community we offer here draws on sociological concepts both to support and to challenge the church's ministry of community formation. Our intent here is not to deny the difficulty of nurturing community in our own time and culture. Rather, this book undertakes a ministry of clarification.

Sociology and social psychology provide a consensus on the characteristics of community as a style of group life. But few non-specialists have access to this information. The goal of this volume is to give access, to make more widely available an understanding of community illumined by the resources of the sociological tradition. The book invites readers to befriend the social sciences so that their power may be put at the service of the mission and ministry of the Christian people.

Befriending involves acquaintance with the perspective from which sociologists and social psychologists view the question of community. Befriending also includes a critical awareness of the limits of the social sciences. Sociology can not resolve the dilemmas of Christian community, but it can help clarify the problems and possibilities that are part of the ongoing experience of community living.

To speak appropriately of the community of faith, we must place the resources of the social sciences in contact with people's hopes and histories and with gospel convictions about community life. Conversation among these three authoritative sources—Christian tradition, personal experience, and contemporary social sciences—can contribute to the building up of the faith community. This volume supports that ongoing conversation.

Within this book, then, we will bring the resources of the social sciences into dialogue with the images and ideals of community life that we share as Christians. Part One discusses elements essential in *forming* the community of faith; Part Two considers theological images *shaping* our common journey; Part Three takes up the dynamics at play in *living* the community experience.

We encourage readers to contribute to this reflection their own experiences of community. Reflective exercises at the end of each chapter help readers identify these experiences—positive and negative—and clarify the convictions born of their experience. The exercises are designed for personal use, but their value is greatly enhanced by sharing them in a small group setting. As we offer our own considerations on the complex question of community, we are grateful for the valuable work being done by many others. At the end of each chapter we provide a selection of additional resources from this wealth of helpful material.

We intend this book for use among a wide range of groups who struggle to understand themselves as community. These include parishes, basic Christian communities, pastoral teams, justice networks, congregations of vowed religious, parish councils and committees, school faculties and boards, faith-sharing groups, health-care systems, recovery networks, diocesan agencies, and movements for political action and social reform. Many (though certainly not all) groups in each of these categories see the religious ideal of community as a model of their life together and as a goal of their interaction. By assisting these groups understand the issues that influence their shared life, the chapters ahead will help shape an effective ministry of community formation.

PART ONE

FORMING THE
COMMUNITY OF FAITH

CHAPTER ONE

WE HUNGER FOR COMMUNITY

Amid our busy distracted lives, we long to belong. Followers of Jesus, we hunger for community, for a home where our faith finds nourishment. We yearn for a gathering that welcomes our gifts and respects our wounds. We long for an assembly that can enkindle our faith in the face of an often cold world.

The search is for more than a haven or momentary respite. We desire to link our lives with other believers and, in these bonds, to be nourished. Many of us desire a deeper connection with our religious past, our birthright, the almost forgotten communion of saints. And we yearn to discover in the random details of our personal lives a meaning and purpose. We struggle to trace the connection between our brief life and the Christian story, to believe that our fragile efforts of charity and justice are part of the plot, vitally linking us to God's own designs.

For some of us, this longing summons images of the first Christians. With nostalgia we recall their enthusiasm for *koinonia:* partnership, commonness in faith. "These remained faithful to the teaching of the apostles, to their shared life (*koinonia*), to the breaking of the bread and to the prayers" (Acts of the Apostles 2:42). The radical union suggested here both excites and frightens us: "the faithful all lived together and owned everything in common" (Acts 2:44).

Drawn together by their shared faith, our religious ancestors felt bound in partnership to God's own spirit: "The grace of the Lord Jesus Christ, the love of God, the *koinonia* of the Holy Spirit be with you all"

(2 Corinthians 13:13). This communal bond among the earliest Christians lowered, for a brief historical moment, the social boundaries of race, status and gender. Among those baptized in Christ, the distinctions between Greek and Jew, free person and slave, female and male would not prevail (Galatians 3:27). In these first communities we hear no hint of hierarchy; separating believers according to power and privilege, from fatherly leaders down to docile children, would be a later development.

These earliest communities knew conflict and survived its purifying touch. Peter and Paul, two strong egos, strenuously disagreed over the best strategy for welcoming non-Jews into the new faith. Having fought and compromised, Paul could say with satisfaction: "So, James, Peter, and John, these leaders, these pillars, shook hands with Barnabas and me as a sign of *koinonia*" (Galatians 2:9).

How to rekindle such *koinonia* in our communities today? The obstacles are impressive. North Americans are individualists: we prize our independence and flinch at any infringement of our privacy. Often we worship in large, anonymous parishes. We meet our Sunday obligation in staid or rushed liturgies, standing next to each other, unknown individualists. We hear the Word of God but remain unmoved; we take Communion but leave unnourished.

Three biases imperil our hopes for a richer life of shared faith. To many of us, church life is "one more thing" to be squeezed into a busy schedule. Religious experience competes on the calendar with job commitments and family care, car pool, and little league. Conversion comes as we reclaim the faith community as a privileged place, a *sacred space* where we find support to sort out these demands, rediscover our perspective, and say no to what is unnecessary or harmful to our life of spirit. Only then is religious living rescued from its perilous status as "one more thing."

A second bias that thwarts shared faith is the expectation that we are to be fed. The Christian laity have been successfully educated to be religious consumers. We come to the church as children; we demand to be cared for. A parish is the place where we bring a baby to be baptized, an adolescent to receive moral instruction, a young adult to be married, a loved one to be buried. (In crasser moments, we might even admit: "This is what we pay for!") We gather to watch the ceremonies; we arrive to receive the sacraments. Experiences like this do not bode well for an adult community of faith, a *koinonia* of mutual responsibility and shared mission.

A third bias taps into the romance of community. Under the weight of religious rhetoric, we come to expect a gathering of believers harmonious and free of discord. We hunger for a community free of conflict, demanding not only unity but uniformity. But the *koinonia* in the early church did not guarantee such an idyllic world. For our deepest hunger for religious community to be satisfied, we will have to face our suspicions about diversity.

Befriending Diversity

For Christians, diversity starts at the beginning. The power we follow is too complex to be captured in a single image; we recognize in God the partnership of creator, redeemer, spirit. In our Scripture, four gospels express one faith. Reading these texts we hear the same story told in different voices. If one of these accounts of Jesus' life is true, are the others false? We remember that this is a story of God entering human life, of a mystery we attempt to describe in the single word "incarnation." We remember too that God is ineffable—unspeakable. Yet we speak this good news again and again. This endless rephrasing of the central mystery of our life is where religious diversity begins.

Church historians show us how diversity has described our shared life from the beginning as well. Jesus' followers in Antioch crafted expressions of belief that were different from those in Jerusalem. During the early centuries of Christianity, our religious ancestors argued endlessly about what it means for Jesus to be Christ, both human and divine. Is he a God who, for our salvation, "disguised" himself as human? Or was he a man, human like us but blessed by God in a way that is unique? This argument is never finished because we touch here a mystery we cannot fully express. Similarly, from the earliest days Christians have debated the means of our being saved: Do we rely utterly on God's grace, or must we make every effort to live in a way worthy of our calling? The answer is, paradoxically, yes. But efforts to appreciate the interaction of faith and works have generated different—sometimes conflicting—understandings.

The richness of our religious history stems from our ability to express, in partial but vigorous fashion, our unfolding vision of our life with God. Instead of clinging to a single unchangeable meaning of sexuality or authority or grace, we search out new images and idioms to say our faith again. In this faithful effort, pluralism is not a scandal but a blessing. Diversity is an essential characteristic of a vital community of belief, a resource to be mined, not a flaw to be overcome.

But this vision of diversity remains difficult to embrace. For many of us, argument and conflict scarred our families of origin. We know, too, that disagreements threaten and sometimes defeat religious community. These painful experiences can lead us to see all diversity as a scandal. We become desirous of a faith life that admits no disruption or confusion. We come to suspect *difference* as a sign of division, even disloyalty. We hope that our religious faith will be a bulwark against the winds of change. We ask of God a clear, unambiguous revelation that finds expression in an undebatable orthodoxy which, in turn, can be communicated in a single, lucid catechism. We hardly notice the wall we are building, the wall that will keep God in place and protect us from change.

Religious diversity thus comes to be a scandal. To some it even appears as a surrender to relativism. Critics raise a cry against "cafeteria Catholics" who believe selectively and choose according to personal whim. (Unexamined in this image is the implication that, like good children, we should eat whatever is put before us and never question the chef.) Indeed, relativism is a strong current in American life. Suspicious of past orthodoxies or simply exhausted by strident public debate, many Americans give in: "whatever works" or "different strokes for different folks." Though we avoid disagreements and confrontations this way, we may also surrender the lively exchange that keeps our faith vitally connected with the rest of life.

Diversity in Service

If diversity begins for Christians in the Scriptures themselves, it flowers today in the experience of mutual service. For many centuries the church was pictured as a hierarchical family in which parental clergy cared for the children of God. In such a world, ministry had a unambiguous meaning: it was the work of the clergy. Vowed religious instructed our children and lay persons helped out in the parish, but it was the ordained pastor who ministered. In the 1960s this clear vision of ministry changed with a surprising suddenness. Lay people started to appreciate their commitments in family life and work as having a deep significance—as ministry. People in all walks of life—teachers and health care personnel, working people and business managers, public officials and artists—began to suspect that their professional tasks and their faith life intersected in a genuine vocation. Our parishes were quickly peopled with professional staff and active volunteers: religious educators, pastoral counselors, justice ministers, liturgists, youth workers, spiritual directors.

This sudden blossoming of ministry among us reminded us of the earliest Christian communities. A variety of gifts marked these original gatherings. The Spirit of God stirred different ones in the community to preach, visit the sick and care for the poor, to prophesy, to organize the group's life. Then an odd dynamic occurred: as Christianity expanded geographically, ministry began to shrink. Gradually over the first several centuries, Christians came to expect those in the official roles of priest and bishop to provide the services a faith community needed.

Expecting much from the priest, we expected very little from ourselves. The community of believers was pictured as a gathering of the ungifted, a passive assembly waiting to be cared for. The explosion of ministries in our recent history has led us to a different vision. We bring to our gatherings not only our needs but our gifts. A parish, we come to see, is rich with ministers, gifted and generous folk willing to support one another and eager to witness their faith in the broader community.

The variety of ministries within the community demands that ministers come together in a new way. The image of the pastor as unique minister, as solely responsible for the group, is being replaced by a team of adult partners in ministry. New ministers arrive not as "father's helpers," but as colleagues and siblings in the family that is the church. Ministers everywhere struggle with the painful challenges of collaboration: learning how to support and challenge one another, how to face conflict, how to acknowledge our needs and limits. As ministry teams learn this new asceticism, their behavior gives witness to what they preach: ministry as a communal calling, as the responsibility of all the baptized.

Diversity Within Belief Itself

Christians have always believed diversely, arguing about Jesus as both human and divine, disputing whether we are saved by our virtuous efforts or only by God's grace. This very diversity fuels our tradition's vitality and longevity. Only recently has diversity broken open the cramped definition of ministry as exclusively the work of those who are ordained. As we become more comfortable with diversity as an indispensible characteristic of religious faith, we gain the courage to admit the diversity within our own faith life.

This threatening pluralism in our faith is experienced in the phrase, "no one believes it all." This is both a simple and unsettling statement. Each of us is gifted with only a partial understanding of the mystery of God among us. Our vision is unavoidably partial, our personal perspective flawed. This limitation in faith becomes clear when we reflect on a community praying the creed. As individuals we may sense that our faith is fragile. But joining our voices in this public confession of faith, we express both the unity and fullness of our belief. Together we say more than we can say alone.

When we look more closely at this public confession, we see a bewildering variety of belief that supports this harmony of voices. One person in the group prays the creed with an intense yet peaceful faith. The person next to her gives his voice to the common prayer with very little attention or conviction. A third person prays in apparent unison but, in fact, struggles against the doubt or despair growing in her heart.

These different voices praying in apparent harmony both represent and disguise differing modes of belief. And this pluralism is often reflected in the heart of individual believers. Today one part of the creed captures our attention since it expresses our present relationship with the Lord. We pray this phrase with great energy and concentration. Later in this same communal prayer we pronounce a sentence that we want to believe, but from which we feel distant. We do not so much deny this tenet of Christian faith as we feel unable to embrace it with much conviction. But others in the group pray with us. In this part of the creed, they pray it *for us.* Their faith supports both our belief and our unbelief.

We see here how a community differs from an individual. A group of Christians believes in a comprehensive fashion that is unavailable to the individual believer. Our shared belief amplifies and completes my partial faith. It encourages my belief and sustains me through my unbelief. In the fullest sense, it is the community that believes.

Relieved of the unrealistic expectation that each of us "believe it all," we can acknowledge who we are: people of faith and unfaith, blessed with strong convictions and bedeviled by enduring doubts. Such a fragile combination is not a peculiar failure of our private faith; this is what Christian faith looks like. This humble recognition can save us from two extremes: the righteous belief that our own faith is fully orthodox and thus the measure of other's adequacy; or the pervasive despair in the weakness and inconstancy of our own belief.

If "no one believes it all," then perhaps "no one believes all the time." The journey of faith leads us more deeply into the mystery of our life with God. But this journey is seldom a smooth ascent. Along the way we take wrong turns, go down cul-de-sacs, get lost. Often our faith grows through disruption and failure and loss. Such a journey will likely include periods of unbelief.

"No one believes all the time." Recently a good friend, a professional minister in the church, suffered a family tragedy. Struggling to deal with this loss, she felt that she no longer believed in God, that she had lost her faith. Listening to our friend's experience, we become aware of three possible responses to her grief. The first and most extreme would be to take this absence of faith literally and advise her that, if she could no longer believe, then she was no longer a Christian. As a non-believer, she no longer belonged in the community of faith.

A second response would be to deny the seriousness of her loss. The temptation here is to assure her, "You haven't really lost your faith. You're just depressed. Everything will be fine!" This is a ministry of distraction; we hope to distract our friend from the gravity of the crisis because we are ourselves so uncomfortable with it.

A third response would take seriously both her loss of faith and the context of the loss: her inclusion in this believing community. First we need to honor her loss. Tragedy has broken her trust in a loving God. But we hold this "faithless" person within the believing group. Surrounded by believers, this woman has time to experience her unbelief and its causes. In this protective environment, she has space to lament and await healing. Meanwhile the community believes for her. Their faith sustains her through her time of disbelief. As she speaks with members of the community, as she learns about their own journeys of faith and unfaith, she sees both their scars and their resilience. Such faith, wounded and mature, predicts to her the future of her own belief.

For this woman, the community acts as a sacrament, witnessing to the possibility of belief even in the face of absurdity. Holding her disbelief, the community believes for her. And in time she begins to believe again, though now in a more mature way. An earlier naive faith dies and from its death comes a more robust commitment to the mystery of God among us. This transformation of faith happens in the midst of a community that believes in her and for her. Gradually the group's faith effects what it signifies: it makes more faith as her belief comes to life.

The expectations that we should believe it all and believe all the time flourish in the cultural soil of individualism. A strength and curse of American national life is the ambition that each person be independent and self-sufficient. In such a cultural climate, we tend to see community as a gathering of well-rounded and self-sufficient adults. Our religious tradition offers us a truer image: community as a gathering that enlarges and challenges and completes our personal vision, a place where both our strengths and our hungers are welcomed.

FOR FURTHER REFLECTION

Consider your own experience of diversity. Recall a group that is important to you—among your family or friends, in your work setting or civic involvement, or part of your life of faith. First, list the similarities you find among people in the group: the sources of the group's sense of unity. Then, list the group's diversity: in experience, in abilities, in values, in attitudes, in goals.

As you see it, are there ways that this diversity has been troublesome in the group's life? Give some examples to show what you mean.

In your experience, are there ways that this diversity has enriched the group? Again, offer some concrete examples.

ADDITIONAL RESOURCES

In *Plurality and Ambiguity* (San Francisco: Harper & Row, 1987), David Tracy examines the dizzying pluralism in contemporary society through the metaphor of "conversation." Tracing the historical process through which hierarchical images emerged to overshadow an earlier diversity in New Testament communities, Elisabeth Schüssler Fiorenza calls for a return to the "discipleship of equals" in *In Memory of Her* (New York: Crossroad/Continuum, 1983). Kevin Giles discusses the origins and development of ministerial roles in the early church in *Patterns of Ministry Among the First Christians* (HarperSanFrancisco, 1991).

Raymond Brown and John Meier explore the different nuances of faith that guided the development of the earliest communities in *Antioch and Rome* (Mahwah, N.J.: Paulist Press, 1982). Brown discusses the tensions and differences within the community that composed the fourth gospel in *The Community of the Beloved Disciple* (Mahwah, N.J.: Paulist Press, 1979); for his consideration of the synoptic gospels, see *The Churches the Apostles Left Behind* (Mahwah, N.J.: Paulist Press, 1984).

Church historian James Hennesey examines the religious pluralism within which Catholicism developed in the nineteenth century and how radically different this American view of diversity was from the prevailing European view of church authority in "Catholicism in an American Environment: The Early Years," *Theological Studies* (December 1989), pp. 657-75; see also Joseph Fitzpatrick, *One Church, Many Cultures: The Challenge of Diversity* (Kansas City: Sheed & Ward, 1990). For pastoral strategies for facing pluralism creatively, see Greg Dues, *Dealing with Diversity: A Guide for Parish Leaders* (Mystic, Conn.: Twenty-Third Publications, 1987), and Stephen Kliewer, *How to Live with Diversity in the Local Church* (Washington, D.C.: Alban Institute, 1990).

The richness and diversity of material on Christology published in the past decade attests to the rich pluralism in this area of theology; see, for example, Bernard Lee, *The Galilean Jewishness of Jesus* (Mahwah, N.J.: Paulist Press, 1988), John Dominic Crossan, *The Historical Jesus: The Life of a Mediterranean Jewish Peasant* (HarperSanFrancisco, 1991), and Elizabeth Johnson, *Consider Jesus: Waves of Renewal in Christology* (New York: Crossroad, 1992).

CHAPTER TWO

COMMUNITY IS A WAY
TO BE TOGETHER

The challenge of community is alive in the church today. Christians unhappy with the impersonality and bureaucracy of official church life look for more significant ways to share their religious life and hopes. Some seek out opportunities for charismatic prayer. Others establish contacts with people who share their concerns for ethics in the workplace or justice in the political arena. Attempting to nourish a sense of belonging and a commitment to ministry, parishes encourage small groups for prayer and study, for recovery and reconciliation, for spiritual formation and social action. Women and men in ministry establish collaborative work groups and peer networks for professional support. Small intentional communities link families and single adults in a common journey of faith. Congregations of vowed religious stress anew the value of their life in common as a sign of the gospel promise of community, and struggle to make this sign a practical reality in their local houses and institutions. Dioceses implement procedures designed to support greater collaboration among bishops, priests, and people. And theologians work to develop an ecclesiology that takes seriously, both in the church's structures and in its self-understanding, the image of the church as the people of God.

These attempts to enliven the sense of community have been neither easy nor very successful. Students of church life offer a range of reasons to explain the difficulty: numbers, apathy, mobility, time, polarization, inertia, even "bad will." The explanation, perhaps, runs deeper.

In *The Pursuit of Loneliness* Philip Slater, a perceptive critic of the American scene, underscores our cultural ambivalence regarding community. On the one hand, many of us long to be part of an identifiable group of people who are bound together by trust and cooperation. Yet, equally strong among us is the influence of our cultural commitment to individualism and the autonomous pursuit of our own destiny. In *Habits of the Heart*, Robert Bellah and his colleagues show how deeply this ambivalence is rooted in American experience, both in our history as a nation and in our values today.

American Christians share this ambivalence. We want the support that comes from being with people who share our deepest values, but we resent group restraints. We want to participate in groups that help us to feel at home in a complex and confusing world, but we distrust group demands and suspect elitism and exclusivity. The religious call to community arises amid these contradictions.

Community: An Unclear Ideal

The term "community" is itself vague and diffuse. To some of us, the word suggests an interdependence reminiscent of the relationships we imagine—perhaps only nostalgically—to characterize small-town America or the ethnically-defined urban neighborhood. Defining parishes by geographic and territorial boundaries supports this "community-as-neighborhood" model. Some of us focus on different connotations of the word "community." Stressing "community-as-support-group," we expect Christian communities to develop close interpersonal ties in an atmosphere of emotional honesty and mutual encouragement. While these two understandings of community are not necessarily opposed, they are not always easily reconciled.

Religious language about community contributes to the complexity. In its official documents, in its liturgical texts, and in its homilies, the church often calls people to community with images of the family: Jesus taught us to call God "Father"; we belong to "Holy Mother Church"; Paul uses the image of husband and wife to describe Jesus' love for the church. As we struggle to live together in Christian community, these family relationships fill our imaginations. But even as these images awaken our deepest aspirations for love, communion and care, they complicate our attempts to translate religious ideals into the concrete practicality of life together.

For many of us, the family is not the most useful image of an adult community. When we think of a family or, more significantly, when we evoke the images and emotions of our past experiences of family life, the most influential memories are of young children growing up in the presence (or absence) of powerful parents. During the years of active childrearing, parents and children are bound together in many significant and satisfying ways, but they are not equals. Considerable care and much love on both sides may mark these early parent-child relations, but these patterns of relating are not appropriate in an adult community of faith.

As we move through adolescence and into more mature adulthood, most of us renegotiate our earlier relationship with our parents and move toward adult mutuality. We try to reestablish connections with our parents as adult to adult. These renegotiated family relationships hold clues to the inclusion and commitment suitable for the adult community which is the church. But the image of family seldom evokes this sense of mutuality among adults.

Even more significantly, in the experience and imagination of most of us, family is part of our private life. Family represents the place of security and privacy where we find relief from the demands of public responsibilities. The family nourishes our subjectivity and permits us to let down our defenses and be ourselves. But community is not about private life; community is a model for social involvement.

Community is more than another name for intimate self-disclosure and emotional support. In most instances, self-disclosure and support are elements of groups that experience themselves as communities, but more is involved. As a style of social life, community points to the possibility of a shared vision that can move us to action in a public sphere and that can be undertaken in a context of mutual concern.

How do we move from the religious image of community as family to workable models of life together in our parishes, institutions, and ministry groups. This question leads us into a discussion of community as a style of group life.

Community: A Style of Group Life

"The goal of the parish council this year is that St. Mark's will become more of a community."

"The entire community will be assessed for the construction of the new road."

"Our family's main concern about moving to a new city is that we will have no community there."

"Three of us in the community are school teachers; the other two sisters are involved in parish work."

"I joined this ministry team for a community; instead, we have become an organization."

"Lord, we gather as a community at your table."

"Community"—the word has many meanings. Often without a precise definition in ordinary conversation, the term has two common uses. Sometimes we use "community" to mark a special quality we experience in relationships. Where a sense of belonging, an awareness of support, a recognition that we have much in common exists, we experience community. When "community" means these feelings of solidarity, we use the word psychologically. But we also name some groups of people—a parish, a neighborhood, a religious congregation—a community. Here the word signifies a style or structure of group life. We might call this the sociological sense of the term. Here our use of "community" points not to experiences of fellowship and solidarity but to a group's formal *structure* or the ways these people come together, apart from their feeling for one another.

These two meanings of "community" are, of course, closely related. We hope to experience closeness and commitment when we live in a community structure. Yet we can separate the *structure* and the *experience* of community: we may experience strong bonds with persons we see only seldom; we may also participate regularly in a community structure devoid of mutual acceptance and lacking in genuine concern.

In this and the several chapters to follow, we will explore the sociological understanding of community as a form or style of group life. We shall examine the patterns (recurring activities, emerging values, developing relationships and leadership styles) that characterize those groups that function as communities for their members.

Community as an Intermediate Group Style

The social life of most adults is complex. As part of several worlds, we participate in a number of different kinds of groups. Helen Rigali, for example, belongs to three groups that are important to her: family, work, parish. For Helen, her family is the most immediate and the most important group in her life. She and her husband have been married for eighteen years. They are raising two teenage daughters and a son still in grade school. Helen is also a longtime member of Holy Spirit Parish. Enthusiastic about the sense of participation that has developed in the parish over the last several years, Helen and her husband share a renewed commitment to this group of Christians.

Recently Helen has gone from part-time to full-time as a sales agent with a large real estate company. Her contract with the firm clearly delineates specific goals and obligations. Even though her work is often tiring, Helen enjoys it and appreciates the opportunity to interact regularly with clients and other sales persons. But the time demands that will come with her new full-time status concern Helen. If her evenings and weekends are no longer free, will she have to cut back her involvement at Holy Spirit? In addition, she senses some discomfort among her children over her being away so much when they are home. While each of these three groups is important to Helen, they all make demands on her energies, her commitment, and her time.

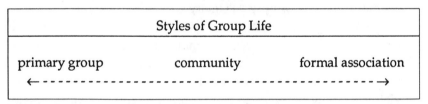

Styles of Group Life

primary group   community   formal association
←- →

Sociologists use the image of a continuum to help us understand the complexity of social life. They extend this continuum from the primary group at one pole (a small grouping with strong ties among members and a wide range of shared interests) to the formal association at the other pole (a more structured organization with explicit rights and obligations). A family, a household, or a close-knit group of friends are examples of primary groups. Formal associations include large organizations, such as General Motors or IBM, and other task-oriented groups, such as a United Way fund-raising committee or, as in Helen's example, a real estate agency.

The word "community" refers to ways for people to be together, patterns of group interaction, that fall in the large middle area on the continuum. It designates an intermediate social form.

Since community lies midway along the continuum, we can expect this style of group life to include some of the elements that are found at either pole. A community is similar to a primary group in some ways, but also different. And, on the other hand, a community has characteristics that make it both like and different from a formal association. In religious discussions of community, we often stress the ways in which community differs from a social organization. Reacting to what we sense was an over-organization of much of church life in the past, we ask community groups to provide what has been missing. We want to come together more spontaneously now, with fewer rules and roles to tell us how to deal with one another. We want to gather in smaller groupings of like-minded persons with whom we feel ourselves emotionally compatible, especially on the religious values that are most important to us personally (worship or justice or spirituality or reconciliation). These two goals stress some of the primary group elements that may be present in the community of faith. But to appreciate the distinctiveness of community, we must also note the ways in which communities differ from the more cohesive patterns of primary relationships.

Community: Not Simply a Primary Group

As a style of group life, community is similar to a primary group in several ways: persons who share community develop emotional ties, the level of personal communication fosters a sense of belonging, and social cohesion becomes important. But a community differs from the model of a family household or other primary group in the following ways: size, intensity, diversity.

Size Primary groups must be small enough to allow face-to-face interaction among all members on a regular basis. Membership in a community need not involve each person in face-to-face interaction with all other members.

Intensity A primary group, due in part to its size, can sustain a high level of emotional exchange and personal sharing among all members. In most cases, this level of dialogue is not a realistic model for personal sharing among all the members of a community.

Diversity The size and interpersonal demands of primary groups both require and produce high levels of compatibility among members. Often one of the reasons that people want regular and continuing relationships with each other is that they recognize similarities: "These people are like me." Moreover, people who spend a good deal of time together and share the same milieu of interests and values tend to *become* more alike over time. The opportunity for—the pressure for— homogeneity among group members is likely to be greater the more close-knit the group. Consequently, coping with diversity is often difficult for a primary group. On the other hand, many groups seek diversity among their members—diversity of experience, interests, perspective, skills, age, or values. A modern hospital or university, for example, would be brought to a standstill if similarity of skills or interests were the prime consideration in who could work there. In many instances, communities require diversity and pluralism to insure their growth, survival, and effectiveness.

Community: Not Simply an Association

As a style of group life, community is also similar to a formal association: the focus of a community (more so than is the case in a family or other primary group) includes values and interests that go beyond the group itself. Thus, the members of a ministry team come together not simply for mutual support but for a task. Interaction within a community requires more explicit understanding of the rights and responsibilities of membership than is the case in a primary group. A potluck supper among a group of friends may succeed with only an informal sense of "who will bring what." However, an effective ministry team requires a clearer awareness of the responsibilities of each member.

But communities also differ in important ways from formal associations. An individual is involved in an organization through a role (for example, as teacher, bricklayer, ticket agent). This role is that part of the person's total self that performs the task or service for which the organization was established. However, involvement in a community is not limited to just one specialized role. Within the community, we can know and share more of an individual's personality and values.

Parish as Community These considerations clarify the sense in which a parish functions as community. Members of a parish share concern for the religious dimensions of their lives: their experiences of God, of prayer and transcendence, of need and justice, of sin and salvation. This religious concern moves members to come together to worship, to explore their awareness of God's movement in their lives, to plan for the religious education of their children, to encourage one another to live and work in the light of the gospel. Because it has a mission, involving members in goals and activities that reach beyond their intimate circle of family and close friends, the parish is like an organization. The congregation nourishes its own religious life so that, by word and deed, it may witness to the saving presence of God in the world. Some parish activities will be structured and made routine—in committees, councils, boards, agencies. Members of the parish take these organizational steps so that their religious purposes may be served more efficiently and effectively. Like organization in business and elsewhere, parish organization often seems to complicate rather than serve the larger goals of the group. However, a parish community without any organizational structure would be without an important foundation for its communication and growth. But the parish community also differs from an organization: our involvement in the parish need not be limited to one specialized organizational role. More of our total self can come into play. Because it allows and even expects personal involvement and commitment among its members, a parish is similar to a primary group.

However, the larger size of a parish, its necessary procedures of membership and responsibility, and an ongoing concern for its mission make parish life unlike primary relationships. A parish community can be made up of a number of closely-knit smaller groupings: families, neighborhood clusters, prayer groups. But the level of friendship within these small groups will differ from the interaction among members of the parish as a whole.

Religious Congregation as Community We may also apply this understanding of community as an intermediate form of group life to a congregation of vowed religious. The religious congregation as a whole resembles a formal association in many ways: it is a legal entity with explicit structures of authority and accountability and stated norms governing the rights and duties (financial and otherwise) of membership. But religious congregations are not simply formal associations.

They are voluntarily formed groups of adults who come together for mutual support in a shared religious vision. To the congregation as a whole, the internal focus (mutual encouragement and challenge) and the external focus (a mission of witness and action in the world) are of matching significance.

But local houses of religious congregations often balance these two goals differently. Some local houses function toward the primary group pole of the continuum, as small, close-knit groups of religious whose principal function is to support and challenge one another in personal and ministerial growth. While each person is involved in ministry, the house does not share a group ministry. Other religious houses attempt to combine both functions. Members share a common ministry (in a health care institution or school or social justice project) as well as a commitment to one another. This living arrangement, while it makes additional demands on all the members, can also provide the advantages of effective collaboration and a strong communal witness. The failure of the attempt to combine common ministry and common residence, however, can lead to frustration both at home and at work.

Ministry Team as Community   A team of colleagues in ministry can also function as a community. Such a group will be small, manifest a high level of social cohesion, and encourage honest emotional exchange among members, all characteristics that move it toward primary group functioning. However, this team will distinguish itself from a primary group in the importance that members give to the accomplishment of their tasks in ministry.

Not all ministry groups are, or stay, communities. If the pull of primary relationships is strong, if members increasingly turn to one another to experience closeness and emotional sustenance, a ministry team may become more like a support group. This is not, necessarily, a bad thing and may be the most appropriate development for a particular group at a particular time. This development entails a movement away from the social style of community toward the social style of primary group.

On the other hand, a ministry team may find the interpersonal issues of their members too distracting, or too time-consuming, or too threatening. Members may opt, consciously or unconsciously, for more formal, limited, work-oriented relationships. The decision to focus the team's interaction more exclusively on the task need not mean that their relationships must deteriorate to the level of anonymity or animosity. But such a decision will move the group closer to the social style of a formal association. Such a group of co-workers may describe their collaboration as that of a staff rather than a team. In some situations this is the most appropriate model for working together in ministry.

Many varieties of collaborative relationships exist in ministry today. Not all of these include, or need to include, expectations of community. But increasingly those in ministry express a desire to be more that simply a well-organized staff. (Often enough, to be sure, those in ministry together experience themselves as a good deal *less* than a well-organized staff!)

Community in Many Forms

The examples we have considered here show us that community takes many shapes. More than one way exists to bring people together, to organize their interactions with each other, to guide their communication, to support their success. Some effective communities—small house churches, for example—look a good deal like primary groups. Members give serious attention to the group itself and hold high expectations of faith sharing and mutual support. Other effective communities—a school faculty, for example—function more as organizations, with greater focus on a goal beyond the group itself and more limited expectations of emotional exchange. A style of community interaction that suits a prayer group of six or eight people will most likely be inappropriate as a model for staff members in a diocesan agency who wish to make their interaction more communal.

"Community," then, is not a univocal term. Within the broad category of those groups that function as communities, we will discover noticeable differences. Some of these differences relate to a group's history. For example, groups that initially are not communities may take steps to become more communal in their style: a primary group of close friends can decide to work together to develop a cooperative day-care center for their children. The group members remain committed to their values of friendship and mutual support. However, they now attempt to supplement these values with a shared commitment to action. At the other pole of group styles, members of a social service agency decide to adopt a more collaborative working style; to support this, they commit themselves to spend some time together each week in an informal setting away from work.

While the social styles that emerge in these two instances may differ considerably, we may consider each a community, an intermediate social form. What we know is that community does not point to one particular structure of group life. Rather, the term refers to a range of social forms, a variety of patterns of interaction and communication within groups. One group incorporates several elements and expectations of primary group. Another shows more concern for formal patterns of organization. But each may be understood as a community, an intermediate style of group life.

Large groupings of religious people, such as a suburban parish or a religious congregation with several hundred members, will inlcude a wide range of group styles. Within this grouping will be primary groups, intermediate communities, and more task-oriented organizations, each serving a different need within the religious life of the group, each being an appropriate style of interaction for religious people. Religious people sometimes think of "community" exclusively in its primary group connotation. But surely the Christian witness of working together unceasingly, even if not always easily, to hasten the coming of the reign of God stands equal to the Christian witness of the love we bear one another as a sign to the world of God's presence among us.

FOR FURTHER REFLECTION

Consider the images and experiences that influence your own awareness of community. Two exercises may help to achieve a clearer sense of these personal meanings.

1. "For me, community is..." In a quiet atmosphere, reflect on this phrase and take notes of the different words and images that come to mind. Writing down your responses helps keep them in mind. Stay with the exercise until you have completed the phrase several times.

Then look back over your responses. What image or understanding of community emerges from your list? Is there a dominant mood or attitude? What do you learn here about your own expectations of community?

2. Next, consider the groups to which you belong, the settings in which you participate with other people on a regular basis. After you have taken some time to list these groups, ask these questions: Is any of these groups a community for you? Which one(s)? What does it mean for this group to be a community?

Spend some time examining the things that indicate community to you; be as concrete as you can. What action or behaviors do you point to? What feelings or convictions are part of your experience of community in this group?

ADDITIONAL RESOURCES

Social analysts have studied the paradoxes and contradictions inherent in our country's cultural commitment to individualism. Robert Bellah and his colleagues draw on historical and current sources to discuss four expressions of individualism that are central to the way that Americans make sense of themselves and their society; see their influential discussion in *Habits of the Heart* (San Francisco: Harper & Row, 1986) and the accompanying book of readings, *Individualism and Commitment in American Life* (San Francisco: Harper & Row, 1987). In *The Good Society* (New York: Alfred A. Knopf, 1991), this group of scholars expands their discussion to explore the role of "the common good."

Philip Slater, in *The Pursuit of Loneliness* (Boston: Beacon Press, 1990), offers a provocative discussion of the strain between community and independence in the American character. In *The New Individualists: The Generation After the Organization Man* (New York: HarperCollins, 1991), Paul Leinberger and Bruce Tucker explore the re-emergence of individualism in the context of U.S. business enterprise.

Religious thinkers examine ways in which these cultural bias can be healed. Rosemary Radford Ruether discusses the significance of women's experience in expanding the possibility of community in the churches in *Women-Church: Theology and Practice in Feminist Liturgical Communities* (San Francisco: Harper & Row, 1985). In *The Different Drum* (New York: Simon and Schuster, 1987), M. Scott Peck examines the lack of effective community in U.S. society, especially in its churches; he observes the self-help tradition of Alcoholic's Anonymous to be a particularly American model of grass-roots community. Dennis Geaney looks at the religious hope for community in *Quest for Community* (Notre Dame, Ind.: Ave Maria Press, 1987). Gibson Winter traces the global changes heralded by movements in support of community and interdependence in *Community and Spiritual Transformation* (New York: Crossroad, 1989). Paul D. Hanson provides a comprehensive sketch of the developing understanding of community through the Hebrew Scriptures to the time of the New Testament church in *The People Called: The Growth of Community in the Bible* (San Francisco: Harper & Row, 1987).

CHAPTER THREE

QUESTIONS THAT COMMUNITIES FACE

A group that wants to be a community has a series of questions to ask. These questions clarify our experiences and expectations about Christian life together. The questions do not elicit a single "correct" answer or point to the "one right way" to bring about community. On the contrary, they help us become aware that communities function in various ways.

We may ask the following six questions about a community:

1. What is the major focus of this group?
2. How fully are members involved?
3. Is emotional sharing encouraged?
4. How is group behavior regulated?
5. How obligated are members to each other and the group?
6. How are group members evaluated?

Our first goal in asking these questions is clarification: we want to understand how a particular group functions. Later we may ask how satisfied members are and whether the group meets the obligations of its charter. But such evaluation must remain a subsequent goal. Our first task is to describe the group as accurately as possible. Here we will consider each of the six questions, giving some examples of how different groups respond.

What Is the Major Focus of This Group?

Sometimes the main reason a group comes together is for the group itself. Activities are directed chiefly toward the needs and interests of the members. Examples here could include a family household, a circle of friends, even a more formally constituted support group.

But in other situations the focus of a group's activities is outside the group: doing a job, making a product, achieving a set of purposes. So, for example, a factory production team, a university curriculum committee, or a hospital fund-raising committee exists to accomplish a task that goes beyond the group itself.

Answering this first question helps us clarify the relative importance of the group's internal life and its external goals. Groups rarely exist any length of time with only internal interests or only external tasks. Some combination of internal and external focus is much more likely. Within the family, for example, parents want to provide an atmosphere of encouragement and discipline to help their children do well in school. A factory supervisor starts up a company softball team because he knows that workers who get along well are both more satisfied and more productive. Finding the balance of internal and external focus is an important part of any group's life. And over its course, the focus of a group can shift. Thus a group of friends (primarily an internal focus) may decide to buy stock together or to collaborate in the renovation of their neighborhood (external goals). Some members of a local Parent-Teacher Association may find, through their collaboration in raising money for the school (external goal), that they enjoy each other's company (internal focus) and decide to vacation together.

How Fully Are Members Involved?

A second dimension of group life concerns incorporating members within the group. The question here is how much of the individual member is available to the group. At issue here is not so much commitment as comprehensiveness: We may feel *deeply committed* to our jobs even if only a *limited range* of our total personality may come into play in the work setting. The "how much" we are examining here, then, is measured more in breadth than in depth.

Before we explore this question in groups, let us note some differences in one-to-one relationships. In some relationships—in a friendship, for example—we may share a good deal of ourself: our ideas and emotions, our memories of the past and our hopes for the future. In other relationships less of our total personality comes into play. With an aquaintance in the neighborhood, we may exchange greetings and, perhaps, other small courtesies: keeping an eye on each other's homes or taking in the mail when one of us is out of town. But neither party wants or expects the relationship to develop beyond this.

Our participation in groups reveals similar differences. Among a group of friends, we bring much of ourselves to the interaction. True, even with friends we may not bring up a troubled relationship within our family and we may honor a sense of confidentiality about some things that go on in our work. But when we gather as a group of friends, we expect the give-and-take among us to cover a range of mutual interests and to include sharing on several levels. "More" of us is available in this group than, for example, in a local meeting of the political party to which we belong. In such a political caucus a more limited range of our personality is likely to become involved. This group engages our interests within a narrower scope. The goals we share with others here may be very important to us (honesty in government, improved local services in our neighborhood, a court system that safeguards basic human rights), but we do not expect to share much of our broader life interests within this group.

In some groups, then, members are more completely integrated and share a wider range of their personalities, talents, values, and emotions (such as in a family, sorority, or commune). In other groups, members are involved partially and instrumentally, through explicit roles (as first grade teacher or committee member or employee). Note that this question does not deal precisely with the issue of personal commitment or the extent of our appreciation for the group. The point at issue is structural, not motivational. We may be a committed member of a neighborhood improvement group: we attend meetings regularly, contribute financially, and volunteer a good deal of time to projects that further the group's goals. However, the group engages only a portion of our larger personality. The weekend party that brings together a group of old friends may lack the focus of a block club meeting, but the get-together has a range of broader personal involvement, at least potentially. The success of the party depends on the wide involvement of group members. And this involvement is not limited to the accomplishment of particular tasks. We need to do more than show up on time with our share of the food. Our friends expect us to be present to them, to contribute to the festive mood, to be available in ways that are difficult to specify ahead of time.

So, raising the question "how fully involved?" does not imply that total involvement is the goal in all groups. In some groups, sharing deeply in each other's lives is unnecessary. As stamp collectors, we may be regular and enthusiastic members of the local philatelists' club. But many parts of our life are irrelevant to our role as stamp collectors and so are outside the group's experience. We are not holding back; the other group members are not inhibiting us. Rather our participation in this group is partial, and correctly so.

In other group settings (as members of a citizens' review board, a jury, an industrial arbitration committee) becoming involved in one another's lives is inappropriate. The success of these group efforts often depends on impartial judgment and independent goals. So we limit our social interactions to insure that our personal lives do not become entangled.

In some church groups, too, personal engagement is limited. To be an effective member of the parish council or the diocesan social justice committee, we do not need to become a close friend of all the other members or spend our free time with them. Ideally, we will not view each other as strangers or enemies, but our collaboration may well have a particular and somewhat limited goal. This limited goal does not mean that our relationships cannot be personally significant. We may, in fact, include prayer as part of our gathering or choose to meet socially from time to time. Our membership in groups like this reminds us of the rich variety of relationship styles that enrich adult life. In Chapter 12 we will discuss in greater detail the ways a variety of styles of communication and care contribute to community.

Is Emotional Sharing Encouraged?

This third question examines the place of emotions in the life of the group. In some groups the expression of feelings is important: for example, among friends, between loved ones, in counseling and recovery group settings. Here, sharing at the emotional level is not only acceptable, it is necessary. We legitimately expect to share the inner world of those close to us. Even as we recognize that self-disclosure is always a gift, we feel disappointed, even hurt, when our friend withholds some special joy or sorrow.

Many of us have had an experience like the following: We spend a pleasant evening with an old friend whom we have not seen for some time. Over a leisurely dinner we get caught up on the details of each other's life. Discussing our jobs and sharing some laughs, we enjoy the evening together. Several days later we learn from someone else that our friend is in the midst of a difficult time in her career. We feel concern for her, but we also feel left out. She did not have to share that part of her life with us, but still we are disappointed. We want to support our friend; perhaps we can do something to help. Most of all, we wish she had trusted us enough to share her distress with us.

In other relationships we do not expect this emotional sharing. In some groups, such an exchange would be out of place. We can all recall the uneasiness we experience in a group when someone moves to a level of emotional communication or self-disclosure that is inappropriate. For example, at a board meeting of a civic group, a member starts to discuss what she likes and dislikes about her psychiatrist, or, at a meeting of the parish school board, a participant begins to share his dismay over his marital problems.

In some groups we expect very little emotional exchange. In other groups, we encourage only positive or only negative emotions. The unspoken code of a group of business colleagues, for example, may permit the exchange of only their success stories. However, a group of teenagers may share only their negative, but not their positive, experiences of teachers and parents.

Some settings impose other restrictions on our emotional communication, limiting the expression of feelings to particular times (holidays, funerals) or to particular places (taverns, locker rooms). Although groups differ in how they deal with feelings, this emotional dimension remains one of the key elements of group life.

How Is Group Behavior Regulated?

A fourth critical dimension of group life concerns the way behavior is regulated in the group. The question here is not *whether* behavior is regulated; our behavior is always influenced by the persons with whom we interact. The question is rather that of manner: *How* is this regulation accomplished? How do members know what kinds of behavior are expected of them?

In some groups, regulation is more implicit than explicit. In ways about which we are not very aware, the group communicates that certain actions or attitudes are acceptable, even desirable, while others are not. No printed list of "dos" and "don'ts" appears; nevertheless, people know what is expected of them. Social control is often achieved like this, through group pressure or the influence of custom and tradition. A smile or a frown, congratulations or ridicule, inclusion or isolation work powerfully to shape the behavior of persons in the group. Through these and other influences, a shared—though largely implicit—understanding of "how we do things around here" emerges.

In other groups, the process of social influence are more explicit. With the intention of making clear the range of acceptable behavior, the members draw up statements of procedure, formulate guidelines, and promulgate laws. Most groups regulate the behavior of members both implicitly and explicitly. For example, the principal gives new teachers a handbook detailing their rights and obligations as members of the faculty; she also urges them to take their lunch in the faculty lounge so they can meet the other teachers in an informal setting and get a better sense of the school's spirit and morale.

To understand any particular group, we need to appreciate the ways in which the behavior of its members is influenced and the degree to which these influences are implicit or explicit. We do not begin our analysis from the premise that either form of influence is better or more effective. A statement explicitly defining the boundaries of acceptable activity will be influential and useful in many situations. Both parents and their adolescent children, for example, may find that putting the rules of the house in writing can lessen the tension between them around questions of discipline. Or the Diocesan Personnel Office may be commissioned to clarify for the entire diocese some of the issues found to be trouble spots between newly-appointed pastors and members of parish staffs.

But this is not to deny the power of a group's unspoken norms or unwritten customs to keep behavior within certain bounds. Each of us can testify to the power of a group's implicit rules. We can remember instances when we changed our behavior or modified an opinion in response to strong, but often unstated, group pressure. Recalling ourselves coerced like this, we may conclude that the implicit regulation of group norms is generally harmful. But the processes of group life are more complex than this. While examples of the negative effects of social pressure are easy to cite, these tell only part of the tale. As most psychologists and many effective leaders know, group influence is an important and necessary factor in most experiences of personal change and growth. True, a group's lively customs may rigidify into useless conventions. But in many groups, this implicit sense of "how we do it around here" remains more flexible and open to development than do many of the group's formal laws and explicit regulations.

How Obligated Are Members to Each Other and to the Group?

In some groups the obligation that exists among members is broad and diffuse. Members have a wide range of mutual responsibilities, some of which are not easy to list in advance. The commitments of the traditional wedding ceremony express this kind of diffuse mutual obligation: "in sickness and in health, for richer and for poorer, until death do us part." In marriage, no list of particular actions defines or limits our responsibility to one another. Rather each of us stands open to do "whatever is necessary" for our relationship to thrive. Over the course of our life together, we may find that our commitment to one another involves us in situations that we could not have predicted on our wedding day. And yet we sense that this openness to unexpected demands is at the core of our fidelity.

Being a parent is another instance of diffuse and broad obligation. In becoming parents, we commit ourselves to a range of responsibilities that we cannot fully understand ahead of time. We may have a sense of some of the emotional and financial resources that are necessary, but we cannot know for sure just what our own children's development will require of us. Will our baby be healthy or sickly, cranky or good-tempered? In school, will she be bright or slow, athletic or artistic, sociable or reserved? These factors, largely beyond our control, significantly influence the shape of our responsibilities as parents.

Close friendship usually includes a sense of diffuse obligation as well, but with a greater expectation of mutuality than is the case between parents and a growing child. We are not likely to sit down ahead of time with our friends and list the rights and duties that come with our relationship. More probably the friendship develops as we become aware of what we give and receive from one another. And as our relationship grows, so does our sense of mutual obligation.

In many group settings, limited obligations exist. Often we specify these explicit limits in a contract or other legally binding form. For example, the employees' handbook issued by many companies attempts to set out clearly the extent of the company's obligations to its employees (often expressed in terms of salary categories and fringe benefits) as well as the employees' obligations of presence and productivity to the company. Other aspects of employees' lives, other needs they may experience, are, strictly speaking, beyond the scope of mutual obligation that exists between employer and employee.

In other groups with a limited range of obligations, the definitions of mutual responsibility remain largely implicit. That is not to say that the scope of obligations in these groups is unclear. For example, even though nothing appears in the bylaws, the members of a parish religious education committee know that in a pinch they may ask for the loan of another member's car. But to ask another committee member for a loan of money would be inappropriate.

In some groups traditionally characterized by diffuse obligations, members are now trying to clarify the range of mutual responsibility. Some couples today draw up marriage contracts that specify their sense of obligation to each other regarding finances, property, children, career, and provisions to be made in the event of death or divorce. Recent developments in religious congregations offer another instance of this move from diffuse to specific obligation. Formerly the event of final vows, following upon a probation period of several years, signaled the religious congregation's assumption of final responsibility for the individual member. The religious in final vows could feel confident that the congregation would provide whatever is necessary, including basic necessities of food and clothing, a place to work and a group with whom to live, required education and medical services, even long-term care in case of illness or debilitating old age. Religious congregations today have moved from this broad and diffuse range of obligations to a somewhat more limited and more explicit set of mutual obligations. Thus, the current documents of many congregations include guidelines concerning the obligations that exist between congregation and member in regard to salary, job placement, living arrangement, the funding of education and preparation for retirement. To some, such a specific statement of mutual responsibilities is disconcerting. This arrangement challenges, even contradicts, their understanding of the congregation as "my family." However, this change does not automatically signal a loss of loyalty between the religious and the congregation. But the psychological and practical repercussions are often significant enough to require a reworking of the sense of mutual commitment.

How Are Group Members Evaluated?

How does a group determine the worth of its members? In some groups we value a member as a result of membership itself: this person is important to our group simply because she belongs; the basis of her worth is that she is "one of us." Loyalty among members is strong in groups like this, as examples from family life show. Preparing for the traditional Christmas gathering, family members realize, "We have to invite Uncle Charlie." Nobody really likes Uncle Charlie. He talks too loud, he drinks too much, he even frightens the children. But he *is* Uncle Charlie, a part of the family. For better and for worse, he is "one of us." He belongs at the family gathering, at least for Christmas dinner.

In other groups, our performance determines our value. The good group member is she who makes an effective contribution to the group's task, he who fulfills well the requirements of his role. And the better a person's performance, the more valued that person is. The more our group is involved in a task or a goal beyond the group itself, the more importance we attach to members' effectiveness and performance. We are likely to be valued by the planning committee to the extent that we contribute to the plan. The more effective we are with troubled teenagers, the more the staff at a neighborhood crisis center will appreciate our participation in the volunteer program.

Many other groups fall between these two types, groups in which both *belonging* and *performance* are used to evaluate members. Sometimes one of these criteria will clearly be more important than the other ("I don't care what her ethnic background is! She does such a good job around here we ought to bring her into the management team."). Sometimes one criterion will be used to mitigate the effects of the other ("I know his sales quota is down again. But he's been with us since the beginning, and we should take that into consideration."). Sometimes the two criteria are in clear conflict ("Brother Paul is not a good principal for this kind of school, but he is a member of our congregation. Shall we keep him in the position, since he is one of us, or shall we give this important position to a more effective 'outsider'?").

Throughout this discussion of the basic aspects of group life, we have noted that each dimension describes not a set of opposing categories into which groups will fall neatly, but a continuum along which groups will range. These six questions provide an analytic framework, alerting us to the underlying issues that are part of community formation. We can recast the questions into a chart and use it to examine the community groups in our own ministry. The chart can be used to describe how a particular group currently functions or to clarify how the group could—or should—perform differently. Using the chart, we must remember that observers may differ in their judgment of where a particular group stands on any one of these questions. And over the course of its history, a group's answers to these questions will probably be different at different times. The more a group appears on the left side of the chart, the more this group can be understood as functioning like a primary group, where priority is given to the group itself and its social cohesion. The more a group falls to the right on the chart, the more it incorporates elements of formal organizations. Here members are likely to place a premium on effective performance and on the achievement of a corporate task beyond the group itself. This analysis of the elements common to all group life serves as a context for our consideration, in the next chapter, of the characteristics of community.

FOR FURTHER REFLECTION

The dimensions of group life that we have discussed in this chapter can be explored in several ways. In the exercises below we suggest four directions in which an analysis may be taken. The questions may be used to clarify your own sense of how a group is functioning now (Exercise 1). Or you may reflect on how other members see the group (Exercise 2). Or you can use the chart to highlight changes (Exercise 3) or to point to problem areas (Exercise 4).

It is not necessary—it may not even be helpful—to undertake all these analyses at once. Instead, start with the first exercise and spend time reflecting on the information that emerges in your response. Plan to go on to other parts of the reflection later, as your time and interest permit.

Questions Communities Face

A. What is the major focus of this group?

group itself $\longleftrightarrow$ 1 2 3 4 5 6 7 its task

B. How fully are members involved?

many parts of self $\longleftrightarrow$ 1 2 3 4 5 6 7 one's role

C. Is emotional sharing encouraged?

emotional depth $\longleftrightarrow$ 1 2 3 4 5 6 7 neutrality

D. How is group behavior regulated?

custom/pressure $\longleftrightarrow$ 1 2 3 4 5 6 7 procedures

E. How obligated to one another?

loyalty $\longleftrightarrow$ 1 2 3 4 5 6 7 contract

F. How are members evaluated?

"one of us" $\longleftrightarrow$ 1 2 3 4 5 6 7 performance

Exercise 1. Select a group to which you belong and consider it in terms of the six dimensions of group life. Ask yourself the questions that appear on p. 28 and mark your responses along the chart on p. 38. For each question, circle a low number if you think that the group acts more like a primary group; circle a higher number if you think that the group acts more like a formal association. As you reflect on the profile that emerges, are you surprised by any of the judgments you have made?

Exercise 2. Now mark the chart as you judge most other members of the group would evaluate it. Compare with your own responses. How do the two charts differ? What does this tell you about your own participation in the group?

Exercise 3. Mark the chart to indicate the way you saw the group when your participation first began. Again, compare this with your current evaluation. Are there significant differences between the two? If yes, why do you think this is so? Has the group actually changed? Have the changes been chiefly in your own awareness?

Exercise 4. Mark the chart to indicate the way you would prefer the group to function. Are there differences between this "ideal" and the way you see the group as it actually performs? In what area does the discrepancy appear?

Inviting members of a group to undertake this exercise together can be useful. Have each person complete the chart, as suggested in Exercise 1, and then discuss together the similarities and differences that appear. The group may wish to complete one or more of the other exercises suggested here, taking time after each personal analysis for discussion within the group.

ADDITIONAL RESOURCES

Excellent resources abound to support communities of faith and those committed to helping community happen. Arthur Baranowski presents a tested program for restructuring parishs into small faith communities in *Called to Be Church* (Cincinnati: St. Anthony Messenger Press, 1990); in addition, see his *Creating Small Faith Communities* and

Pastoring the "Pastors": Resources for Training and Supporting Pastoral Facilitators, also available from St. Anthony Press. In *Small Christian Communities: A Vision of Hope* and the accompanying *Resource Book* (Mahwah, N.J.: Paulist Press, 1991), Thomas Kleissler, Margo LeBert, and Mary McGuinness draw on their experience in the phenominally effective RENEW program of parish renewal to provide guidelines for supporting small faith communities.

In *Good Things Happen: Experiencing Community in Small Groups* (Mystic, Conn.: Twenty-Third Publications, 1992), Dick Westley reflects on the hopes and hungers that bring people to small faith communities. William Bausch offers both encouragement and practical advice in his *The Hands-On Parish: Reflections and Suggestions for Fostering Community* (Mystic, Conn.: Twenty-Third Publications, 1989). In *Living the Faith Community* (Minneapolis: Winston Press, 1985), John Westerhoff sets out a practical vision of the church as community. See also the expanding list of faith-sharing resources incorporating scripture, prayer, and group reflection, available in the Small Group Resource Series (Kansas City: Sheed & Ward).

The increasing interest in the development of communities of faith is reflected in several national networks of small faith communities. We list their names and addresses here, encouraging readers to be in direct contact with one or more of these groups.

Buena Vista, Inc.
Network of Small Christian Communities
P.O. Box 5474
Arvada, CO 80005-0474

Sojourners Outreach
Faith Communities for Justice
P.O. Box 29272
Washington, D.C. 20017

National Alliance for Parishes
Restructuring into Communities
P.O. Box 1152
Troy, MI 48099

North American Forum for Small
  Christian Communities
c/o Rosemary Bleuher, National Chair
430 N. Center Street
Joliet, IL 60435

Communitas
Intentional Eucharistic Communities
P.O. Box 4546
Washington, D.C. 20017

In addition, annual conferences provide opportunities for members of small faith communities to exchange experiences and resources. Contact the organizations below for further information.

"We Are the Church" Conference
Small Faith Community Caucus
Call to Action
4419 Kedzie Avenue
Chicago, IL 60625

Communities of the Future Symposium
Benet Hill Center
2577 N. Chelton Road
Colorado Springs, CO 80909

Ministry Center for Catholic Community
540 N.E. Northgate Way, Suite 141
Seattle, WA 98125

CHAPTER FOUR

What Makes a Community?

Whenever people discover they share significant concerns, a basis for community exists. These common interests move people to come together to discuss, to plan, to act in common in light of their concerns. Community begins in this context of communication and commitment to common goals. But a community cannot long persist unless its members appreciate diversity within the group and display a willingness to face the conflicts inevitable in any sustained relationship.

In Chapter Two, we introduced the understanding of community as an intermediate style of group life. Communities operate neither simply as primary groups nor exclusively as formal organizations; instead, they function in ways that fall between these two styles. In this chapter, we expand our discussion of this intermediate style, seeing it not simply in terms of what it is not (neither a primary group nor a formal organization), but in terms of its own particular characteristics.

Within the sociological discussion, five characteristics describe communities. As a social style, a community is a group characterized by:

1. common orientation toward some significant aspect of life
2. some agreement about values
3. a commitment to common goals
4. opportunities for personal exchange
5. agreed upon definitions of what membership entails.

1. Common Orientation Toward What Is Significant

Community is not a trivial pursuit. Community happens around matters of importance. And since people differ with regard to what is important to them, we must recognize that different people move toward community around different issues. What is important enough to one person to provide the enthusiasm and energy needed to deal with the many complications of being together as community may not be nearly so important to someone else. For example, many people in our parishes find religious practice significant in their lives. Celebrating Sunday worship, participating in the sacramental life of the church, gathering for shared prayer and study—these activities *matter* to them. The formation and nourishment of community among these believing people is the focus of much parish-based ministry.

But for many people today, including a good number of those within our parish boundaries, these religious activities are not a basis for community. The difficulty of building community in our parishes may well be due to factors of size or distance or the complexities of modern life. But another reason may be that parish ministers inappropriately expect most parishioners to find regular participation in the activities of the local church to be of compelling interest. This simply is not the case.

But other facets of life can serve as the focus of community. For example, childrearing issues are of great significance for most parents today. What patterns of love and discipline, of presence and absence, of "mothering" and "fathering" should they develop within the family? How are these patterns appropriately expressed; when should they change? Couples and, increasingly, single parents ask these questions of themselves. Many would respond eagerly to opportunities to share their concerns, to discuss the dilemmas and delights of parenting that they experience, to discover and weigh, in an atmosphere of support and accountability, the options that are open to them. A group formed around these shared concerns for parenting could easily move in the direction of becoming a community.

Other aspects of life also serve as the focus of community: commitment to social justice, concern for nature and the environment, the struggle to overcome addiction, shared interest in the arts. However, not all these concerns provide a basis of community for everyone. What is significant in our own lives determines how we will participate communally with others. Efforts at community development will be short-lived and superficial if they are not grounded in issues of vital personal significance to the people involved.

2. Agreement About Values

Among members of a community, *some* agreement about values is likely, even necessary. If those in the parents' group we mentioned above, for example, find that they disagree significantly (whether "children should be seen but not heard" or "children should be treated as equals in the family") they are not likely to function very long as a community. In another setting, with other values at stake, these same people might work together quite well. For example, even though they disagree about parenting they may share a commitment to preserving their common ethnic heritage and work well together in a Hispanic-American community organization.

A community, then, is a group characterized by some *agreement* (but only *some* agreement) about values. As a social form, community need not require total conformity on value questions. True, a group functioning communally is likely to share many values. Community members tend to see many issues the same way, especially issues central to the purposes of the group. But the overlap is seldom complete. Areas of importance, where group members differ, will always remain. A community's future depends in part on the members' ability to accept and harmonize these differences in ways that contribute to rather than distract from their life together.

The question of shared values is especially volatile in the parish or other religious community. The church today is in a time of staggering cultural transition. This has resulted in wide divisions within what we once thought of as a unified body of believers. A religious group can function as a community only if the members agree on the basic values of their religious experience. In parishes and other religious settings today, many groups lack this sense of congruence and seem polarized over questions of religious meaning and practice.

Efforts to help these groups experience themselves as communities of faith must pay attention to the value gap. An approach that starts in the attempt to mask differences ("We are all saying the same thing") or to legislate the end of polarization through enforced conformity (either "liberal" or "conservative") is likely to miscarry. In some instances, the value disagreements may be more apparent than real; then clarification can be a good place to start. But basic to the healing process is an attitude toward diversity and conflict. A community's ability to move beyond polarization toward a more mature expression of shared belief depends on an experience of reconciliation. Leaders who appreciate the range of values among members, who show a patient confidence in the group's larger unity, and who help groups face conflict, model attitudes that contribute to reconciliation.

3. Commitment to Common Goals

A third characteristic of a community is a commitment to common goals. Communities, more than primary groups, include a focus of concern that goes beyond the group itself. Within groups that function communally, the members demonstrate interest in, even enthusiasm for, action that expresses their values. Members of communities act together in pursuit of the goals and ideals they share.

The parish, for example, is a community for action. Persons come together in the parish in order to accomplish, in ways they could not do alone, their goal of loving God and neighbor. If accomplishing our religious purposes in the parish becomes difficult or impossible (if, for example, parish organizations seem too outmoded to serve as the vehicle of our religious commitment to justice, or if liturgical changes seem too great to permit our expression of worship), participation in parish life can be seriously undermined. A parish community is not likely to develop without significant common goals; the community is unlikely to endure without effective common action.

Some congregations of vowed religious feel a similar loss of common purpose or shared goals. Members report that their corporate goals were clear when most of them worked in institutions staffed by congregational members. However, they wonder what sense of purpose unites the congregation now, when members are involved in a variety of ministries, with some working alone and outside any explicitly religious auspice. In community chapters and other congregational assemblies, members explore the shape of the shared goals that sustain them now and craft policies that will support this sense of common purpose.

These first three characteristics of community groups—common orientation, congruent values, and shared goals—remind us that community involves knowledge as well as love. Community invites its participants to shared activities of evaluation and planning as well as to common actions of acceptance and support.

4. Opportunities for Personal Sharing

A fourth characteristic of communities is the opportunity for personal sharing. A group that wants to function as a community must develop ways for members to communicate with each other at a personal level and to express their mutual care and concern. This can be done in many ways.

Different communities have different expectations of personal sharing. For example, although both groups may function as communities, the level of sharing in a priests' support group is likely to be different from that among the executive committee of the parish council. A prayer group's expectations about mutual support differs from those of the staff of a diocesan justice network, but in both groups mutual support may be important. Thus, the gift of mutual concern is offered and received in different ways. Ministers of Christian community must sensitively support the expressions of personal sharing and concern appropriate to a particular group.

In communities, we must not leave the development of these appropriate patterns of personal communication to chance. While we can overdo a group's concentration on its internal communication, most groups err in the other direction. They neglect to develop and nurture opportunities for members to share with one another at both intellectual and extrarational levels. Honest, direct communication among members is essential in a community. But equally and often even more important is the opportunity for celebration, both in the sense of ritual and recreation. Our community rituals (shared prayer and commemorative events and party festivities) engage us at a level beyond our formal goals and explicit purposes. These moments of celebration nourish a sense of communion and solidarity among us. An enhanced awareness of our unity (community in the *psychological* sense) contributes significantly to the more ordinary processes by which we work out our ongoing relationships within the group (community in the *sociological* sense).

As we have mentioned before, the self-disclosure of deep friendship is not a necessary norm of personal exchange in every community. But some appropriate and generally satisfying pattern of personal exchange must exist. Groups that do not pay attention to the quality of interpersonal exchange and do not give time to activities of mutual support will not long survive as communities.

5. Agreed Upon Definitions

A final characteristic of communities is agreed-upon definitions and shared expectations about how the group operates. Members want to know how the tasks of the community are divided up and what is expected of them. Clarifying the group's patterns of leadership and authority becomes important. The group needs common understandings of the responsibilities an individual assumes by becoming a member of this community as well as common understandings of how the various responsibilities within the group are related to one another.

Each of the five characteristics of community discussed here is an important, even essential, ingredient of any group that wants to be a community. But in the experience of many people, problems regarding mutual expectations are a troublesome obstacle to community formation. All of us are likely to have our own definitions of an active parish, a successful house church, a dedicated ministry team, a model religious house. Each of us carries, at least implicitly, a sense of what should go on within a community. These expectations serve as guidelines that influence our behavior and offer us criteria by which we can judge ourselves and other people. Complications arise, however, when we live together, work together, and share our experience of faith—with slightly differing images and ideals of cooperation, authority, and leadership. The problem is not diversity. As we have suggested earlier, diversity, within certain wide margins, is a potential resource for community. The problem is that we do not acknowledge and appreciate these differences.

An example may prove helpful here. For you, community means that people who work together in ministry turn to each other first for support and companionship. The work that we do together is important to you, but you see it as a result rather than a source of our deeper commitment. For me, community means that we are both motivated in our work by the call that the poor have the gospel preached to them. I care about you as a colleague and respect you as a dedicated minister, but I do not expect us to become close friends.

Our differing expectations of community are not, of themselves, a problem. If we are each aware of what we expect in community, and if we can make these expectations clear to one another early, we can come to some mutually satisfying understanding of what we can realistically expect of one another (and ourselves) in our working relationship this year. We may come to appreciate the other's point of view, seeing it as enlarging our understanding of community. Or we may realize that our differences are substantial enough that we are not able to function as a community. While we remain together in this ministry setting, our expectations of one another become more modest. But in either case, this clarification has served our collaboration.

However, when we do not acknowledge differences in expectation, they remain just below the surface, until such time as they erupt as irresolvable points of divergence and conflict. For example, having gone for several weeks or months on the assumption that "we all want the same thing" in our team meetings, we can become distressed as we begin to realize this is not so. For you, the goal of the team meeting is to assure that the multiple responsibilities of ministry in the parish are assigned and carried out. You are convinced, however, that the demands of both ministry and personal maturity require that we function autonomously as we accomplish our tasks. I am convinced that any *real* team must be committed to group discussion and consensus decision making; often, in my judgment, coordinated action will be necessary as well. So I resist your attempts to streamline our meetings by delegating responsibility quickly and leaving individual team members to make their own decisions concerning their ministry. I begin to see your style as abrupt and even manipulative. You, in turn, may interpret my resistance as disruptive of pastoral effectiveness or as an attack on your leadership.

The conflict that often becomes inevitable at this point may serve the team well. Our antagonism makes clear some of the different ways a team can function. Out of the controversy that ensues, we may come to a better sense of who we are as a team and how we want to be together in ministry. But often conflict does not have this good effect. Rather than seeing the controversy as a signal that we need to clarify differing expectations, many of us respond to the emotional force of the argument, interpreting it simply as a clash of personalities or seeing it as a sign that our collaborative effort is doomed.

In summary, we need to note several things about conflict, a powerful and often confusing dynamic in community. First, community life does not do away with conflict among us; some conflict may be expected and even be valuable in the life of a flourishing community. Second, not all conflict in groups is useful; some kinds of dissention can lead to the disintegration of a group or end its effectiveness. Third, one way a group can deal effectively with conflict is through efforts at clarification.

The process of clarification, then, is central to community. Clarification is an ongoing requirement, important not only at the outset but as a continuing part of group life. During their formative period, groups are wise to discuss the hopes and intentions of the members, the roles and responsibilities that each will undertake, the patterns of authority and communication that work best. But change and development are as much a factor in group experience as in personal life. Unless we continue the process of clarification, regularly or periodically, we may not remain alert to the changing images, expectations, and needs that occur in the life of our community.

Ministry of Clarification

Throughout our discussion we have returned often to the themes of diversity and pluralism. We have maintained that pluralism can be an important resource for community. But we can also experience pluralism as a source of complication and confusion. Our realization of this ambiguous function of diversity calls for further comment on the ministry of clarification. Clarification is an important initial step in the formation of a community of faith. This ministry of clarification takes several forms. First, we must make explicit the "oughts" and "shoulds" that we use to evaluate the community. Often these value criteria remain implicit, not fully available to us or to others. We are not suggesting here that these implicit personal standards are invalid. Rather, when these criteria remain implicit and solely personal, misunderstanding and frustration frequently result.

Second, the sociological categories we have examined can themselves be used as tools of clarification. An awareness of the basic dimensions of group life as presented in Chapter Three can sensitize us to the role of these elements in our own group, whether this be a parish, a ministry team, or a small faith community. Examining a particular group in terms of these dimensions will often provide deeper understanding, sometimes even new information, about the group. The six questions that guided our analysis in Chapter Three can direct our attention to aspects of the group's life that are central to its functioning. An examination of a community in terms of these categories can help us recognize the group's strengths and diagnose its limitations.

We may undertake this examination of a community in common. Group members, for example, can reflect on the exercises at the end of each chapter in this book and share their responses with each other. Where attitudes of honesty and acceptance prevail, this discussion can highlight areas of agreement, disclose differences in expectation, and reveal issues of potential concern. This exercise can result in an agenda for action to enhance the group's life as a community. In addition, many people report that the attempt to clarify their expectations, with an opportunity to share this experience with the group, is itself a community-building event.

A third clarification concerns the costs of community. Community is not free; we pay for the benefits of social cohesion in the coin of personal accomodation and compromise. Any relationship asks that we give up some areas of our independence. This is the price we must pay if we seek genuine interdependence. Our early enthusiasm for community may mask these costs. Initially we experience only the benefits of being together: support, inclusion, communion, shared goals. But a group whose members do not have a capacity for generous self-disregard cannot sustain these benefits. Participation in community should not require us to annihilate ourself or to give up all personal responsibility. But we can expect that participation in community will make real demands on us. All the members of our group must understand the costs that characterize our community. These costs differ from group to group. Within a group, we will experience differences as well: a compromise that is acceptable to one member may seem an unreasonable demand to another. The recognition of these differences does not, of itself, resolve them. We will need to go beyond clarification in efforts to negotiate, to come to a mutually acceptable resolution of the differences that exist. But in negotiation, too, clarification is an indispensable first step.

Vision of the Community of Faith

A vision of the community of faith emerges from our sociological analysis. We shall discuss this vision here, using the parish as an example. The vision is equally relevant to other expressions of religious community.

The parish is a local body of believers whose religious hope manifests itself in their ministries of service and sacrament. Since its goals include both an internal and an external focus, the parish appropriately develops the social forms of community. The parish is meant to nourish and express the communion that exists among its members. But this is a communion in meaning and mission as well as in fellowship. The experience of communion results from and is sustained by an awareness of shared meaning and a participation in a common mission. The mission of the parish has a focus beyond the parish, as this local body participates in the task of the whole church: to witness to the world the saving presence of God among us.

For many, participation in a community of believers provides a social setting that assists them in mediating among the conflicting value systems in which they are immersed through their daily life and work. The religious community can support us as we struggle to establish a sense of priorities reflecting our religious commitment. By supporting the development of a lifestyle in which our deepest values can be shared with others and expressed in common action, such a community serves as a context for personal integration. The community of faith is thus a social network that challenges people to personal conversion (values) and sustains them in their attempts to live out (behavior) the implications of this conversion. From personal transformation, committed religious action flows.

In the end, the formation of the community of faith remains the work of the Spirit. A well-structured group, clear in its goals, open in its communication, committed to its religious values, may still founder. Life remains that ambiguous; faith, that much a mystery. But being aware of the social dynamics of group life and sensitive to the particular history of this group can contribute importantly to the possibility of community. And the possibility of community is the hope in which we stand, awaiting God's gracious visitation.

FOR FURTHER REFLECTION

Use the five characteristics of community discussed in this chapter to reflect on your own experience. Select a group that serves as a community for you. Consider each of these questions in turn, taking time to allow yourself a full response. Noting down your responses may help, since each questions is likely to prompt several comments.

1. What is the significant area of life this group is concerned about? Is there more than one area of significance?

2. What values do you, as members of this group, hold in common? Are there significant values members differ about? How important are these differences in the group's ongoing life?

3. What are the goals and purposes of the group? In what ways do members act together to accomplish these goals?

4. When and how do members spend time together? What kinds of personal sharing is encouraged? How satisfying are these patterns for you? for others?

5. Are members clear about what is expected of them here? Do members know what to expect from one another? Make a list of what is expected of people who belong to this community, as you see it. Which of these expectations seem valid to you? Do any of these expectations seem invalid?

When you have completed these questions, look back over your responses. Do any of these areas seem to be "trouble spots" for the group? What actions might be taken to strengthen the group in each area?

ADDITIONAL RESOURCES

Religious research and sociological analysis alike contribute to a clearer understanding of the shape of small communities of faith. Robert Banks discusses the historical context of the early house churches to which Paul ministered in *Paul's Idea of Community* (Grand Rapids, Mich.: Wm. B. Eerdmans, 1980). Focusing on religious communities, Mary Wolff-Salin explores negative dynamics in small groups in *The Shadow Side of Community and the Growth of Self* (New York: Crossroad/ Continuum, 1987). Juan Luis Segundo examines the challenges of community to instititional religion in *The Community Called Church* (Maryknoll, N.Y.: Orbis Books, 1973). In *Ecclesiogenesis* (Maryknoll, N.Y.: Orbis Books, 1986), Leonardo Boff draws on the Latin American experience to describe the role of basic Christian communities in the transformation of church structure.

Consulting the classic sociological tradition on the form and function of groups that can legitimately be called *communities* can give the religious reader a new perspective. We list here several authors who have contributed significantly to that ongoing discussion. In *The Sociology of Community* (Glenview, Ill.: Scott, Foresman, 1973), distinguished sociologist Jesse Bernard provides a useful discussion and critique of what she judges to be the "four classical paradigms (that) encompass most of what we know about the sociology of community." Robert D. Boyd summarizes his comprehensive theory of small groups in "A Matrix Model of the Small Group," *Small Group Behavior* 14 (November 1983), pp. 405-418 and 15 (May 1984), pp. 233-250. Robert Nisbet traces the use of *community* as a sociological category in the work of important nineteenth-century founders of the discipline in *The Sociological Tradition* (New York: Basic Books, 1966), pp. 47-106; see also his *The Quest for Community* (Berkeley: Univ. of California Press, 1990).

In *Contemporary Community: Sociological Illusion or Reality?* (New York: Harper & Row, 1973), Jacqueline Scherer draws upon the evidence of contemporary research to explore the experience of community in the structures of modern life; she includes a chapter on the parish. Maurice Stein, in *The Eclipse of Community* (Princeton, N.J.: Princeton University Press, 1972), considers what has been learned about the structures of community life from the tradition of community studies in American sociology; his interpretive chapters in Part III are particularly valuable. Anthropologist Victor Turner discusses the contributions to an understanding of the psychological experience of community (his *communitas*) to the structure and vitality of group life: see his *The Ritual Process* (Ithaca, N.Y.: Cornell University Press, 1969) and also "Passages, Margins, and Poverty: Religious Symbols of Communitas," *Worship* 42 (1972): 390-412 and 482-494.

CHAPTER FIVE

COMMUNITIES AND A LARGER WORLD

To be in community is to belong. Many of us hunger for this experience. We want to be part of a close-knit group where sharing and emotional support are strong. Since communities nurture solidarity, looking there for support makes sense. But community is about more than solidarity. In communities we are concerned about what goes on among us *and* about the larger purposes that bring us together. Communities, then, have both an internal and an external focus. Concentrating exclusively on experiences of support (the psychological sense of community) can be misleading. Focusing on the emotional advantages of belonging to a community sometimes distracts our attention from the group's broader potential.

Perhaps we expect so much emotionally from our communities because acceptance and belonging seem so hard to find elsewhere in our lives. Friendship, for example, promises solidarity and support. A friend is someone who knows us well, a person to whom we can reveal ourself and who is open to us in return. Having a close friend—someone with whom we can share confidences and upon whose affection and concern we can depend—is one of life's richest experiences. In fact, psychologists today affirm what many of us already know from personal experience: a capacity for friendship is an important indicator of emotional maturity; the presence of a close friend enhances well-being and increases life satisfaction. With real friends, we are both stronger and happier than alone.

And yet, friendship is not frequent. Many adults, perhaps even most, sense that the demanding responsibilities of their careers and families make nurturing friendships difficult. And yet friendships rarely flower without nurturing. Close relationships take time. Developing a friendship requires continuing contact in an atmosphere that lets us feel secure in ourselves and safe with one another. But most settings that bring us together as adults do not offer such security. Our deep-seated cultural commitment to individualism leads many Americans to view their neighbors as strangers and their co-workers as potential rivals. Competing with those among whom we live and work makes friendship risky. We may be courteous and even sociable, but we are not likely to become real friends.

If friendships develop at all, this is more likely to happen in private. In *Seasons of a Man's Life,* for example, psychologist Daniel Levinson notes *first* that the experience of close friendship is rare in the lives of the men he studied and *second* that when a man did speak of having a close friend, he usually mentioned his wife. (Perhaps equally important to note, however, is that many men in this study did *not* experience their wife as a close friend.) The work of social psychologist Lillian Rubin, reported in her book *Just Friends,* discusses the significant differences between women and men in the place of friendship in their lives. But both Rubin and Levinson concur that for a good number of American adults—men and women, married and unmarried—genuine friendship is, in Levinson's words, "largely noticeable by its absence."

If friendship, then, is rare so also is a sense of effective participation in society. Perhaps we do not really "belong" here either. Most people today do not feel engaged in the larger world of their own society. Take voting behavior as one example. Continuing a downward trend from the mid-1950s, barely half the adults eligible voted in the presidential election of 1988, less than 40 percent in the congressional elections of 1990. When asked why they do not exercise this core right of democracy, many people report a conviction that their vote makes no difference. Recognizing that social and political developments affect their lives, they nevertheless feel powerless to influence these events. They see themselves more as "patients," those to whom things are done, than as participants, those who act in the public sphere. This sense of estrangement deepens the division between public and private worlds.

Feeling that we are not really involved in our own society results in social alienation. We may identify our alienation as *normlessness:* we are not sure what to do, what is being asked of us by our society. Or as *meaninglessness:* we have no sense of shared values; the goals and purposes that seem to motivate other people are irrelevant to our life. Or as *powerlessness:* we are unable to control our own destiny; we have no way to influence the important events of our world.

Feeling alienated, some people look to a small community not as a way to become involved in the larger world but as an escape from it. In part, the recent upsurge of interest in religious fundamentalism and other sects is traced to this desire for group support in the face of a confusing and even hostile public world.

Recognizing this reclusive tendency in some small groups, people concerned about public life and social action are often suspicious of community formation. They berate intentional communities and self-help groups as too often and too easily absorbed in narrow internal concerns. Within the churches, for example, faith sharing groups and recovery networks are sometimes accused of focusing too much energy on personal issues. Their critics insist that such self-absorption is scarcely compatible with the gospel's call to a mission of justice and mercy.

Other people, looking at the evidence from grass-roots community organization and the basic community movement, see these intermediate groups as strengthening rather than distracting from public participation. The church's experience in Latin America, the Philippines, and elsewhere shows that involvement in small faith communities can move individuals beyond a sense of isolation and impotence. In *Dangerous Memories: House Churches and Our American Story,* Bernard Lee and Michael Cowan demonstrate the power of such intentional communities to challenge the individualism that often erodes religious experience in North America. These new house churches and alternative parishes provide settings in which Christians can both clarify their values and find support to act on them together.

When we understand small groups primarily as sanctuaries from the difficulties of public life, we distort the goal of community and underestimate its power. By reinforcing the break between public and private life, this view compounds the underlying problem of alienation. Worse, such an understanding distracts us from seeing communities as groups that can effectively link us with society rather than shelter us from it.

Public and Private Worlds

A profound split between "public" and "private" characterizes modern society. The distinction between these two realms of human activity, however, has a long history. Social analyst Hannah Arendt has shown that the political theory of classical Greece sees the public world as an arena of pluralism: participating in public life means experiencing a range of diverse activities and competing values. Public life is also open to public scrutiny: all citizens, each from a slightly different perspective, can see and judge what takes place in public. Thus, what we do in public takes on a meaning that goes beyond personal motives or private intentions. Public activities stand on their own. What we do and say "in public" become part of a shared world that is larger than just ourself. Moveover, the effects of our public actions may sometimes be quite different from what we expect or intend. When we "go public," we enter this network of interaction that we cannot completely control.

In this classical understanding, private life, in the family or household, is a *privation*. What are the "deprivations" of private life? The private world is marked by the absence of other people. In a family or household we are not necessarily alone, but the range of our social interaction is limited. As the Greeks saw it, this restricted sphere deprives us of experiences essential to life and of relationships necessary for the development of our highest capacities.

The private world, the home of intimacy, is crucially important to our life. Personal preferences and ties of affection shape private relationships, nurturing our subjectivity and combating a debilitating sense of isolation. But this subjective focus can be limiting. Within our private world, we are without the social identity that comes from being seen and heard by those who are not our intimates.

Private life may be "off the record" but public behavior is open to public comment. Other people will interpret (and sometimes misinterpret) what we say and do in public. Thus our public identity, the social significance of what we do, reflects more than our personal motives. In that sense, our social identity is more "objective" than our personal sense of self. Our public activities also put us in touch with a wide variety of people, many of whom we do not personally choose. Instead, we deal with other people in the context of a common society in which we all participate, even if our goals and values differ. These public relationships, less based on emotional ties and personal preferences than those in our private life, again take on a more "objective" quality.

The private world can also deprive us an an important experience of achievement. What is done in private often remains without social significance or consequence. Many women feel this deprivation keenly. Women's contribution in the North American labor force in now indispensible; women's participation in the political arena has increased dramatically; women's presence in the professional arenas of law, medicine, science and business is taken for granted. And yet the prevailing cultural norms still see the private world as women's proper place. Women expend much of their creativity and energy on tasks of family and home that are central to the private sphere, but that continue to be judged by public criteria as without significance or economic value. This imbalance does not lead most women to repudiate the private world. Rather, they are becoming aware that the private realm is only part of human life, only part of their own lives. Increasingly, women are chosing to complement their commitments in the private world with social roles and activities that place them more firmly in the web of public reality.

Retreat From the Public World

Where do we make a difference? Do other people care about the things that we think are really important? How can we make a contribution to more than just ourselves? As we mature into adulthood, these questions carry us beyond our circle of close relationships: our family and friends. Pursuing a sense of personal competence and social identity moves us into the public arena. But if participating in this larger world brings failure—if we find no way to really get involved, if what is important "out there" seems far removed from our own life or beyond the scope of our influence—then we pull back from public involvement.

Consider these examples: A minority skilled worker senses that the leadership of the union local is as much the enemy as is the company management. A young manager comes to realize that because she is a woman she will not be promoted to any position with real policy-making responsibilities. A political activist finds that his values concerning citizen participaton are irrelevant to the processes the party uses to select local candidates for public office. In each case, the person's response may well include a retreat into private life.

Frustrations experienced in the social world may bring us back to our private life with heightened expectations. Feeling disconnected and defensive in the public arena, our activities there bring little personal fulfillment. But here, among our intimates, we feel safe. Here we are not anonymous. Here—and perhaps only here—we make a difference. Only here do we have any sense that our actions count. Not surprisingly, then, we look for personal meaning and fulfillment in our private life.

But achieving meaning in the private realm alone is not easy. As important as the world of intimacy is, it is not the whole of life. When we look for fulfillment in private, we often find only disappointment. To develop fully, we normally need to transcend (though not repudiate) the private world. Expanding our capacity to care is one sign of this transcendence. As we mature, the boundaries of what really matters to us expand to include more than just those things that directly touch our own life. Increasingly, we become aware that "our kind"—those who have some claim on our concern and resources—are not just our family and close friends. This sense of responsibility may lead to our personal investment in broader social issues: not just improving our child's school but working for a better educational system; not just keeping property values stable in our neighborhood but working for decent housing for low income families in our city.

Signs of this maturity emerge in our concern for the well-being of a world that will outlive us. Hoping to make the future better, we use our personal resources to influence decisions that are being made now. We get personally involved, even though we will not live long enough to benefit directly from the results. Contributing to a future that is better—for our children, for our children's children, for the children of the world—is reward enough.

The challenge to use our personal resources responsibly in the service of interests that go beyond ourself is central to psychological maturity. Private purposes and narcissistic identity are not enough to carry us to this level of development. Our circle of intimates may inspire and support our involvement in the larger world, but the public world tests and strengthens our resources for generous participation.

But often the public world seems closed to our participation. Expressing our values or exercising our influence there seems impossible or out of place. The objectivity of the public world may provide a sense of order, since its demands are not likely to change from day to day or be subject to personal whim. But often we experience its objectivity as alien. The public realm is not responsive to our interests as individuals; it does not bend to human concern; it does not support personal goals.

One response to the harshness of the public world is to expand our investment in private life. We spend more time on our hobbies or with our small circle of friends; we focus our energy more exclusively on things that will directly benefit us and our loved ones. The paradox of this approach, however, is that we cannot overcome the sense of alienation by retreating into a private world. Withdrawal only intensifies our feelings of isolation. We can overcome social alienation only by finding a way to participate in the public world.

Moving Beyond Social Alienation

Communities help us overcome this alienation. As we have seen, communities are intermediate forms of group life. Neither as private as a primary group nor as public as a formal organization, a community offers a kind of in-between experience of what participating with other people means. The people who share community with us are not limited to only our intimates. Communities offer greater diversity, a range of interests and breadth of purpose going beyond a circle of close friends. On the other hand, communities—as intermediate groups—support deeper relationships than does the public realm. In our communities, we know we belong. Individuality (our own experience, our particular talents, our personal vision and sensitivity) remains important. We contribute to our communities not just in anonymous roles, but because of who we are.

We may find communities like this in a parish setting. The members of the social ministry committee, for example, are not all close friends but over the months they develop a sense of commitment to one another. Their early struggle to understand what kinds of concrete action the group should take has paid off. And while members still experience times of confusion and disagreement at their meetings, most people value what they have learned from the group's diversity. The committee has not been successful in all the projects it has undertaken, but members have discovered that even their failures are instructive. Belonging to a group has made experiencing defeat easier. People have supported one another in facing controversial issues. Being able to depend on other members has been reassuring. Many members comment that, on their own, they would not have gotten involved in these complex problems. But within the group, the issues become more manageable. Coming together regularly also helps keep their sense of commitment high.

Communities, then, function as intermediate groupings, linking the public and the private realms of our lives. Involving members in social settings broader than the family, communities move us beyond the psychological and social limitations implicit in private life. An intentional faith community, the leadership team in a religious congregation, the lay ministry network in a diocese, a faith support group among professional women—groups like these have both an internal and an external focus, both a public and a private face. Occupying this intermediate space, these groups play a mediating role; they link us with the larger world. Vibrant communities involve us in significant exchange with those who are not members of our smaller circle of intimates. Participating in a community challenges us to be concerned about issues that go beyond ourself.

A community, then, gives us a place to stand as we confront the larger questions of public life. By humanizing these concerns, by helping us decide what can be done, by supporting collaborative action, communities strengthen our links with this larger world. Participating in such a community encourages us to deal with the public world, to influence it, perhaps even to change it.

FOR FURTHER REFLECTION

Consider your own experience of the private and public realms.

1. What groups or relationships are chiefly a part of your private life? List the people who are with you in this way.

2. What groups or relationships in your life do you see as part of the public world for you? Again, list these relationships and groups.

3. Does any group play a *mediating* role for you, providing a sense of belonging and at the same time helping you participate in the larger social world? How does this happen? What are the particular ways this group supports and challenges you beyond your private life?

4. Of the groups that you listed in your responses above, do you consider any of these a community? Why or why not?

ADDITIONAL RESOURCES

In "A Church That Turns Outward to the World" *(Origins,* 16 [October 23, 1986], pp. 329-341) Cardinal Stephen Kim of Seoul, South Korea, underscores the importance of small faith communities throughout the world in showing the church the path to its renewal through genuine dedication to the needs of society. T. Richard Snyder calls the people of God to look to their societal responsibility in *Once You Were No People: The Church and the Transformation of Society* (New York: Crossroad, 1990). In *Living No Longer For Ourselves* (Collegeville, Minn.: Liturgical Press, 1992), Kathleen Hughes, Mark Francis and their associates reaffirm the intrinsic relationship between worship and justice in a community of faith.

In *Linking Faith and Daily Life* (Washington, D.C.: Alban Institute, 1991), Robert Reber offers a practical program to assist communities in taking a wider focus in their religious lives. See also John C. Haughey, *Converting Nine to Five: Bringing Spirituaity to Your Daily Work* (New York: Crossroad, 1989) and William E. Diehl, *The Monday Connection: A Spirituality of Competence, Affirmation, and Support in the Workplace* (HarperSanFrancisco, 1991).

James Fowler expands his analysis of stages of personal faith development in *Weaving the New Creation: Stages of Faith and the Public Church* (HarperSanFrancisco, 1991), challenging the Christian community to greater openness to the world and the future. Carl Dudley outlines effective strategies to help faith communities broaden the scope of their ministry; see his *Basic Steps Toward Community Ministry: Guidelines and Models in Action* (Washington, D.C.: Alban Institute, 1991). In *Spirituality for Active Ministry* (Kansas City: Sheed & Ward, 1991), Corita Clarke provides valuable resources for drawing spiritual nourishment from a vital engagement with the public world.

Hannah Arendt examines the historical roots in classical Greek thought of cultural tension between the public and private realms in *The Human Condition* (Chicago: University of Chicago Press, 1958). Parker Palmer challenges religious groups to move beyond goals of intimacy to work more consciously as a force for the renewal of public life in *The Company of Strangers: Christians and the Renewal of Public Life* (New York: Crossroad, 1981); see also his *The Active Life: A Spirituality of Work, Creativity and Caring* (HarperSanFrancisco, 1990). In *The Political Meaning of Christianity* (HarperSanFrancisco, 1991), Glenn Tinder reflects on the prophetic stance required of all followers of Jesus.

The National Center for the Laity provides resources for Christians grappling with the implications of their religious commitments in the public world; see, for example, William L. Droel and Gregory F. Pierce, *Confident and Competent: A Challenge for the Lay Church* and the booklets in the *Spirituality of Work Series,* all available from ACTA Publishers in Chicago. We explore the maturing of personal power through generative care for the world, in our *Christian Life Patterns* (New York: Crossroad, 1992).

CHAPTER SIX

COMMUNITIES
AND SOCIAL CHANGE

Communities offer many benefits. They provide a sense of belonging, connect us with the larger world, and enliven our commitments in faith. In this chapter, we examine another contribution: communities as vehicles of social change.

Communities and Change

One tradition in the social sciences sees community as a conservative force resistant to change. In personal experience as well, many people know that the groups to which they belong have held them back or presented obstacles to significant personal development. A young adult senses that her family and close friends to not want her to pursue the career for which she is particularly gifted. They belittle her ambition and press her, instead, to marry soon and start a family. A pastor resents the pressure of his clerical colleagues who urge him to go slow in implementing a program of effective lay leadership in the parish. An office manager is ostracized by her co-workers when she questions the implicit racism of current personnel policy. In each of these cases, a person seeking change experiences the inhibiting force of a group.

But this is not the whole story of the relationship between communities and change. Group support has sustained many of us in times of personal challenge. Faced with serious personal illness, the loss of a job, or the death of someone we love, we know we could not have lived through the crisis without the understanding and encouragement of our friends.

The connections between community and personal change are strong. Religious traditions recognize that faith has communal dimensions. While religious conversion involves personal transformation, it is seldom achieved alone. For conversion to mature into a new way of living, new believers must become part of a believing community. Their new and fragile faith is nurtured in relationship with these other believers. Among Catholics, for example, the renewed Rite of Christian Initiation of Adults bears compelling witnesses to this conviction.

If connections between community and personal transformation are strong, so are those between community and social reform. Throughout history, people coming together in solidarity and acting together to achieve their goals have spearheaded significant social change. The labor movement, the peace movement, the environmental movement found their earliest strength in groups of people who shared a vision of how things could be different and were willing to act together to effect that change.

Dynamics of Social Change

Social transformation sometimes starts at the top, initiated by people in positions of institutional power, such as a political leader or a corporate officer or, as the actions of John XXIII demonstrated, sometimes by a pope. The purification of church structures begun in Vatican II was largely top-down reform. Bishops listened to the hopes and demands being voiced in communities of faith throughout the world. They consulted theologians, opening themselves to the influence of contemporary research in scripture, liturgy, ministry, church history. Then from their leadership positions in a hierarchical structure, they forged guidelines and enacted legislation that altered centuries-old patterns of Catholic practice.

Grass-roots organizations approach social change from another direction. Grass-root movements draw their members not from those highly-placed in the power structure, but from the folks defined as outsiders: those without much institutional clout, people less likely to be in a position to influence organizational structure directly. Familiar examples show us the pattern: the civil rights movement in this country, the Solidarity movement in Poland, Third-world movements of empowerment among the poor, the women's movement now of international scope. These efforts begin at the bottom, drawing their strength, paradoxically, from people seen by others and often even by themselves as lacking the power, or even the right, to bring about change.

In *Powers of the Weak*, social analyst Elizabeth Janeway explores the connections between community and social change. She begins by tracing a path that many groups committed to social change and institutional transformation have followed. Across a range of different issues —women's liberation, the rights of ethnic minorities, consciousness-raising among the poor and disinfranchised, lay empowerment in the church—similar dynamics emerge. When people talk about their experiences in these groups, they commonly report a series of stages through which individuals—and the group—have moved.

Disbelief

Social change begins in disbelief. To initiate change we must disbelieve that the way things are is the way things have to be. If we cannot question the status quo we remain powerless to alter it. But questioning the status quo means challenging authority, an action most people find difficult.

Many of us move into adult life wounded around authority. From early experiences in our own families and from messages reinforced in our society, we develop an image of authority as external. We picture authority as residing in important institutions and in special people but not in ourselves. This wounded vision of authority results in a world divided between the strong (those who occupy high-status roles and consequently "have" authority) and the weak, which is the rest of us without effective social power.

But as Janeway reminds us, the strong, those who are socially dominant, do not possess their priority outright. The privileged position of those in authority rests on an acceptance of certain definitions of how things are, an acceptance not only by the authorities but by the rest of us as well. To exercise authority, those in leadership roles must be accepted by the rest of us as legitimate. Legitimacy does not necessarily mean that we see a leader as the best person for the job or even as the person we would have chosen. But legitimacy means that we accept this person's influence over the rest of us as in some way justified. In this sense, it is we, "the weak," who confer power on "the strong."

The power of disbelief, then, is tied to legitimacy. In granting legitimacy we accept the current definitions of who has power among us and why. More important, we accept the definition of our own position as weak. Social change begins as we start to question these reigning definitions.

Recent events in Eastern Europe dramatize the power of disbelief. When a people refuses to accept its leaders as legitimate, more and more of the resources of power must be focussed on defending the right to rule and quelling social discontent. Experience in East Germany in 1989 and Romania in 1990 shows that even when leaders command considerable physical force that can be used to compel acquiescence, the loss of legitimacy signals the end of a regime.

The most radical act of disbelief—radical in the strictest sense in that it goes to the root of a society's arrangement—is refusing to accept the way that those in power define us. The strong have defined us as the weak. They see us, and urge us to see ourselves, as without power, unable to determine our own lives, not competent to influence the decisions that in turn influence our world. In disbelief, we start to question *their* right to define *our* experience. Ultimately, we come to see that the definition of ourselves as powerless is a self-inflicted wound. We have colluded with the status quo by accepting its image of reality, by agreeing to its claim that we are weak. Recognizing our collusion gives us options. Our social impotence is not just something that "they" have been doing to us; we have been doing it to ourselves. And we can stop doing it. We can refuse to go along with the image of ourselves as simply bystanders. And seeing ourselves differently enables us to act differently.

Disbelief is the dawn of liberation; social transformation starts here. Our uncritical loyalty to the way things are begins to erode. We recognize that the way things are is not necessarily the way things *should* be; not the only way things *can* be. Disbelief releases creativity, freeing us to imagine alternatives to the status quo. And imagining alternatives is the first step toward their becoming possible.

Coming Together
Social transformation moves to a second stage as we find strength by coming together. Disbelief empowers social change, but disbelieving is

not easy. Trusting our own experience is difficult when it contradicts what most people seem to accept. Sometimes our new awareness contradicts even what we used to accept as normal and necessary. Early in our own disbelief we are tempted to think, "If I'm the only one who sees things differently, maybe I'm the one who's crazy. Perhaps its just my problem." And the status quo has much to gain from keeping the problem personal. As long as our distress is a private matter, there is no cause for political alarm. Personal solutions will be sufficient. We can take a vacation or take a pill, join a health club or see a counselor. The powers that be may even come to our aid, offering resources to help us fit in once again. It is not altruism alone that motivates this institutional generosity. A savvy power structure knows that therapy is always cheaper than social change. A person spending considerable energy dealing with "my problem" is unlikely to bother the people in charge. Underlying definitions remain unchallenged; current structures remain in place.

Social transformation demands that we not disbelieve alone. Joining with others helps the new awareness to grow strong, even in the face of opposition. At least we are not crazy! These other people feel like we do, they have some of our questions, some of our concerns. We have found a group where we belong.

Coming together like this is the next step in social change. Often at first we gather mainly for mutual support. Our common pain connects us. Many groups at this point do not yet have a shared vision or a commitment to common action. These will be important later, as we face the challenge of what to do. But at the start, shared disbelief is enough.

Disbelieving, we come together. And joining together, our power expands. A heady conviction energizes the group. We know we are many and our cause is just. At this stage, solidarity is the group's greatest strength.

And group members are eager to preserve this strong feeling of mutuality. The challenge for a group at this stage, then, is dealing with its own diversity. Disbelief links us in what we are against. But for effective social action, we have to know what we are for; we have to struggle toward a shared vision.

Developing a shared vision confronts us with our differences: the pluralism in our values, our diverse personal gifts, different levels of commitment among us, our different hopes for change. And at this stage, facing the group's diversity is difficult. Admitting that differences exist can shake our sense of solidarity, even threaten the group's continued existence. Rather than confront this inner conflict and risk disintegration, a group may consolidate its identity around mutual support. This is one the right choices a group can make about its own development. In a hostile social environment, safe refuge and mutual concern are no small accomplishments. A support group can be part of social transformation: strengthening its members, healing wounds that linger, confirming a new, more powerful, sense of self, encouraging individuals as they seek change in their own spheres of influence. In this scenario, the group supports the individual as the individual acts for change. But many grass-roots groups move toward another scenario, choosing to act corporately for change.

Shared Action

"Coming together is the bridge that stretches from dissent to common action," Janeway notes. Our solidarity gives us a sense of strength; now we want to do something together about what we believe in common. The vision that emerges among us is crucial here. Our shared dream must be large enough to embrace the group's diversity, significant enough to call forth its courage, and practical enough to offer real hope of success. The decision for public action marks a critical transition. Two questions confront a group at this stage: 1) what kind of joint action should we undertake? and 2) when we turn our efforts outward, will we lose more than we gain? Let's look at this second question first.

Many groups experience considerable strain in the turn toward common action, as they struggle for both inner cohesion and outer effectiveness. Members already know the benefits of belonging and solidarity. Now, if it is to undertake actions for social change, the group must organize itself and its resources. We have to decide on tasks and agree on our respective roles and responsibilities. Lines of authority and accountability need to be sketched; patterns of communication and decision making have to be determined. Without these structures the group's efforts will lack much focus and force. But the group cannot let these structures of effective action develop in ways that destroy its sense of solidarity or its experience of mutual support.

To be effective in social change we must remain concerned about both the quality of our life together and our success in changing the ways things are out there. This dual concern sometimes introduces considerable strain into the group, but the strain is a necessary dynamic in the grass-roots effort for social transformation.

The other critical issue is what shape our shared action should take. At this stage, groups often experience tension between being a movement and being an organization. Movements emerge around a compelling moral vision; organizations form around an effective plan of action. No necessary opposition exists between these two. Movements and organizations are not mutually exclusive, but there is a difference in emphasis.

Movements generate members and commitment by witnessing to values. Much of the action that movements undertake is symbolic: anti-nuclear activists pour blood on missile silos; in Beijing, Chinese students raise a statue in Tian An Men Square to the Goddess of Liberty. Symbolic action makes a value statement. The intent is not so much to accomplish a goal as to draw attention to the deeper issues involved. This heightened awareness of values makes it difficult for a movement to negotiate. Engaging in the give-and-take of political compromise seems too much like giving in or going along.

An organization, on the other hand, has the flexibility to negotiate. With a visible leadership structure, a defined membership, and a public statement of purpose and goals, an organized group can become a direct participant in the complicated process of forming coalitions and forging compromises that advance structural reform.

For a movement, as Gregory Pierce notes in *Activism That Makes Sense*, symbolic action is an end in itself; it tells the world where we stand. For an organization, action is a means to an end. That end is to bring the existing power structure to recognize a new player on the field: this grass-roots group that must now be a part of any decisions that affect its life and its concerns.

What confronts a community at this stage is not an either/or choice, whether to be a movement or an organization. The ongoing challenge, rather, is how to honor both the demands of its moral vision and its goals for practical action.

Community in the Dynamics of Social Change

Social transformation begins in disbelief, draws strength by coming together, and bears fruit in common action. To be an effective movement for change, the group's goals must include both solidarity and positive action or, in our own terms, both belonging and purpose. Groups that succeed in this dual focus develop patterns similar to those we have discussed as characteristic of communities. To undertake action for change, we must organize ourselves and our resources. This involves our coming to some agreement about tasks and roles and responsibilites among ourselves. But we cannot let these patterns develop in a way that destroys our sense of shared vision or our experience of mutual support. Both solidarity and effectiveness remain priorities in our action. As a group, we are concerned about both our life together and our success in changing the way things are "out there." This combination of both internal and external goals characterizes a community more than a primary group or a formal organization.

Not every community, to be sure, will be concerned about social change. But as a style of group life, community can support goals of both solidarity and effective group action. These two dynamics, often experienced in tension, are basic to the sustained effort required for either revolution or reform.

For Further Reflection

Recall the ways in which you have been involved in efforts of institutional reform from the bottom-up (for example, in the political system, in your career or work setting, in the church), or in social transformation (for example, the peace movement, the struggle for social justice, the women's movement, support for the civil rights of minority groups).

Select one of these involvements that has special meaning for you. Recall something of the history: how you got involved, where that involvement took you, who were the people with you in the effort, what outcomes or results strike you as significant.

Finally, identify two or three convictions that you take from this experience, insights about the connections between community and social change.

ADDITIONAL RESOURCES

Elizabeth Janeway discusses the contribution of "coming together" to the processes of social transformation in *Powers of the Weak* (New York: Alfred A. Knopf, 1981); see also her *Improper Behavior: When and How Misconduct Can Be Healthy for Society* (New York: Wm. Morrow, 1987). In *Toward a Christian Social Ethic: Stewardship and Social Power* (Minneapolis: Winston Press, 1985), Prentice Pemberton and Daniel Rush Finn stress the significance of community in social change; see especially Ch. 9, "Empowerment through Small Disciplined Communities." Robert McAfee Brown and Sydney Thompson Brown draw together Christian and Jewish reflections in *A Cry for Justice: The Churches and Synagogues Speak* (Mahwah, N.J.: Paulist Press, 1989). In *Still Following Christ in a Consumer Society* (Maryknoll, N.Y.: Orbis Books, 1991), John Kavanaugh outlines a spirituality resilient enough to support the ongoing effort of involvement in social transformation.

Sergio Torres and John Eagleson reflect on the transformative power of faith communities in *Challenge of Basic Christian Communities* (Maryknoll, N.Y.: Orbis Books, 1988). Rosemary Radford Ruether discusses the role of small communities in the reform of the institutional church; see *Contemporary Roman Catholicism* (Kansas City: Sheed & Ward, 1988) and *A Democratic Catholic Church* (New York: Crossroad, 1992). In *Change Agent Skills* (Monterey, Cal.: Brooks/Cole, 1985), Gerard Egan presents a developmental model to guide a systematic effort to purify organizational structures. John J. Walsh underscores the essential connections between changing people and changing structures in *Integral Justice* (Maryknoll, N.Y.: Orbis Books, 1990).

Gregory Pierce outlines the elements of effective community organization in *Activism That Makes Sense* (Mahwah, N.J.: Paulist Press, 1984). In *Moving Faith Into Action* (Mahwah, N.J.: Paulist Press, 1990), James Lund and Mary Heidkamp provide a practical guide for supporting small groups in a faith-based involvement in social transformation. Kimberley Bobo lists resources and strategies for effective group action in *Lives Matter: A Handbook for Christian Organizing* (Kansas City: Sheed & Ward, 1986).

PART TWO

SEEKING TOGETHER
THE KINGDOM OF GOD

CHAPTER SEVEN

THE DREAM
OF THE KINGDOM OF GOD

The crowd gathered around the old woman. Someone in the back asked, "to what would you compare the kingdom of God? For a long time there was silence. Then the woman said: "The kingdom of God is like a sound. It is the most natural sound in the world. Its melody plays through the hollow places in trees and mountains and people's hearts.

"Jesus could hear this sound approaching. 'Listen,' he would say, 'the kingdom of God is at hand.' He heard this sound playing in children, among the outcasts, when friends gathered to share a meal. Jesus kept moving until he reached a place where he would find its rhythm; then he would sit down and listen.

"The kingdom of God is like a sound. It is the most delicate melody in the world. External noises drown it out; internal rumblings mask it. We hear it for a moment or a day, but then it is gone.

"No one of us can produce this mysterious sound on our own. But we can hunt out the places and people where it plays. We can search for the frequency of its transmission. When we find this sound, we have but to hum along."

After the woman finished speaking, the crowd remained silent for a long time, listening.

A Christian community is not a passive place where individual believers assemble. Our gatherings are crucibles of faith and doubt, of courage and complacency. The mood and spirit of these groups encourage, or inhibit, the continual conversion required of those who follow Jesus. Christian communities support us on this journey of faith by linking our lives in a shared response to God's blessings. The biblical blessing—God's ambition for a world transformed by justice and love—has traditionally been expressed in the metaphor of the kingdom of God.

Many people today, uneasy with the image of *kingdom*, struggle to find a better translation of the scriptural *basileia tou theou* (Wisdom 10:10, Mark 1:15, Luke 17:21, and elsewhere). For some, the word "kingdom" congers up images of outmoded political styles and portrays God as a masculine monarch. A number of theologians prefer the phrase "reign of God"; this image highlights God's on-going influence in our world but avoids the implied masculine bias. Others suggest the word "horizon" to better express the transcendence of God's activity. The appeal of this image is its very ambiguity: we glimpse a horizon without ever reaching it; it beckons us and guides our travels, without falling under our control. Yet for many people, "horizon" remains too sophisticated or abstract an idea. While the search continues for a contemporary image to better express God's elusive force in our life, we will use the traditional phrase "kingdom of God."

Sense of Christian Vocation

A Christian vocation is a calling, an invitation from God to do something special with our life. This calling stirs in the early hopes and dreams that move through our imagination. An ambition to become a nurse or doctor signals our enthusiasm for healing; a hope to become a police officer or lawyer reflects a concern for order and justice. Christians have long believed that such strong stirrings are more than the fruits of genes and environment. These hopes point us toward a life-calling, a vocation. For believers a vocation is a personalized dream; we believe that God quickens our imagination with ideals and ambitions; we experience ourselves being led, called, and even coaxed to live our life according to gospel values.

Over the past several centuries in Catholic usage, "vocation" was interpreted narrowly to refer to the lifestyle of the priest or vowed religious. These were the people, we came to believe, who had vocations. Other Christians were beloved by God but were not called to life choices of any great religious significance.

Today Christians recall that every vocation is rooted in Baptism. When we are joined to a faith community, we are called to follow Christ. And this is not a generic invitation. The call is heard in those stirrings in our own heart that lead us toward lives of commitment with others and service to the world.

A Christian vocation is not something that we *should do*, visited on us from the outside. This calling alerts us to who we most want to be. A vocation-as-dream is a life ambition that can energize different plans and jobs; this abiding hope strives to survive the detours and losses in our life.

Such a vocation and dream grows slowly. Some childhood hints grow into the convictions of the young adult; other glimmers of a future career disappear or are rejected. Through our imagination God speaks to us with many invitations and challenges. A vocation is not a single, clear call at the beginning of adulthood, but a life-long conversation. Even after we have established the patterns of our commitments and careers, God continues to speak, calling us anew and challenging us in unexpected directions. A Christian vocation is, in fact, a gradual revelation: God slowly reveals us to ourselves. At age twenty-one, for example, most of us are not strong enough to bear the full information about our life over the coming decades. God, being of a benevolent persuasion, reveals us gradually to ourselves.

The idea of dream seems especially suited to clarify the growth of a personal vocation. Both a dream and a vocation are fragile, slowly developing life ambitions. Each is an exciting hope for our life, even when vague or in need of care and purification. Each is strangely independent of our planning and control: our deepest hopes lead us beyond safety to new adventures.

Our religious hopes do not grow in isolation. We do not pursue our vocations in private. Our initial hopes as a child were powerfully shaped by the dreams and despair of those around us. As these ideals draw us toward an adult life, we search for others with whom we can share our dreams. Coming to a Christian community we hear about a mysterious, ancient dream: God's own ambitions for this world. Christian communities open to us the dream of the kingdom of God.

Vision of the Kingdom of God

A common dream has been guiding the religious hopes of Jews and Christians for more than three thousand years. Abraham sensed that he was being invited to leave his ancestors' home in search of a new land and a different way of life. This hope stirred in his imagination; he sensed God speaking to him. In Abraham's vision, our own religious ambitions were born. Hundreds of years later his descendants, having escaped from Egypt, would remember this promise to Abraham. Was not this God of Abraham the one who now rescued the Hebrews from slavery and excited them with this hope for a secure and prosperous homeland? In the aridity of the desert, our religious ancestors pictured this dream as "a land rich and broad, a land where milk and honey flows" (Exodus 3:8). Nonbelievers might say this was an hallucination, generated by a desert sun, but to the ancient Hebrews, this unlikely hope became their common vocation.

This hope that flowered in the desert had several characteristics. First, this was a collective dream, a life ambition that belonged to a group of people. Second, it was a dream received as a promise from One they would come to call Yahweh. This dream was not their own invention; it did not originate in them, but came from God. Third, however they would interpret this dream, its energy would continually call them out of the present toward a new and more just future.

The vision of a land flowing with milk and honey seemed, at first, to be fulfilled in the new land of Israel and the kingdom that David and Solomon ruled. But as social injustice and the abuse of power grew and as Israel's infidelities to God's covenant multiplied, our religious ancestors came to see that their shared dream was far from realized. In fact, the very greatness of their state and their kings distracted them from God's holy purpose.

As Israel matured through failure and conversion and more failure (the usual route of maturity), prophets appeared to re-excite the people to their collective dream and to further purify their hope. Isaiah and Jeremiah insisted that this dream of an idyllic place "flowing with milk and honey" must also include a privileged place for the poor, the widowed, and even the stranger. Isaiah (1:16-17) envisioned a society in which care and justice replace the ancient ritual sacrifices:

Take your wrongdoings out of my sight.
Cease to do evil. Learn to do good.
Search for justice. Help the oppressed.
Be just to the orphan. Plead for the widow.

In such a transformed society, people "will hammer their swords into plowshares, their spears into sickles. Nations will not lift sword against nation, there will be no more training for war" (2:4).

But Israel did not heed the challenges and dreams of Isaiah, Jeremiah and the earlier prophets. In the year 587 B.C.E., Jerusalem was conquered and the Israelites were driven into exile, their dreams shattered. In the second part of the book of Isaiah, written during this period of desolation, the writer announces a new and powerful dream: the vision of a servant of Yahweh, a savior who will heal and restore the nation's life. Isaiah (42:1) invites the exiles to hope again:

Here is my servant who I uphold,
My chosen one in whom my soul delights.
I have endowed him with my spirit
That he may bring true justice to the nations.

The dream, begun in Abraham's ambition to find a new home and revived in the Hebrew's vision of a land flowing with milk and honey, was undergoing a powerful transformation. This collective hope could no longer simply be identified with a national state, nor could it exclude the poor and distressed. In their experience of the Exile, the Israelites were again forced to revise, to re-envision their shared dream. Would this future place of justice and love be more interior than exterior, a realm founded more on personal conviction than on territorial sovereignty?

In the centuries between the Exile and the time of Christ, a new and powerful mood swept through the Middle East. A sense that the end of the world was near turned many religious imaginations to thoughts of another world. Perhaps the Jewish hope for a land transformed by justice would not be realized in this world, but in a life beyond the grave, a truly "heavenly" land. During this period the phrase "kingdom of God" made its appearance in the Hebrew scriptures. Wisdom, the feminine voice of Yahweh, assists the virtuous person: "She showed him the kingdom of God and taught him the knowledge of holy things" (Wisdom 10:10). During the centuries just before Christ, Jewish debate continued about the location of this future society and wielded a powerful influence on the first generations of Christians.

In the New Testament, Jesus' ministry begins with the announcement: "The kingdom of God is at hand" (Mark 1:15). Jesus urges others to live with greater love and justice so they will be worthy of this new world that is about to appear. The transformation that this God-shaped world promises is the substance of Jesus' Good News.

The kingdom of God seemed so close to the Jews of this time that even Jesus is ambiguous about whether it is already here. During his final supper with his friend, Jesus announces that he will not eat or drink again "until the kingdom comes" (Mark 14). But when questioned earlier about the signs of its coming, Jesus had responded "You must know that the kingdom of God is among you" (Luke 17:21).

The charm of God's dream for us is its very closeness: now we see it, now we lose sight of it. Like God's presence in our lives, we sense it for a time, then we lose it. Jesus tells us where we can recognize the kingdom's arrival: "The blind see again, the lame walk, lepers are cleansed, and the deaf hear, the dead are raised to life, the Good News is proclaimed to the poor" (Luke 7:22). To Jesus these are both signs and the concrete actions by which this collective dream becomes a reality. Toward the end of Matthew's Gospel Jesus tells his listeners how to act if they wish to be part of this transformation. We are already entering this dreamed-of future when we acknowledge Jesus in the most unlikely places. "I was hungry and you gave me food; I was thirsty and you gave me drink; I was a stranger and you made me welcome; naked and you clothed me, sick and you visited me, in prison and you came to see me..." (Matthew 25:35-36). These actions of justice and love, of caring for "one of the least of the community" usher us into the kingdom of God. This transformation is God's to give, but our actions lead us toward this shared dream.

The gospels are accounts of Jesus' effort to join his personal hopes to the dream of the kingdom of God. Yet, despite his enthusiasm for this vision, Jesus was himself surprised and dismayed by its development. Although he came to Jerusalem sensing danger, it was only in the garden of olives that he realized how radically different were God's plans for him. There Jesus confronted the frustration and failure of his life ambition. His dream of many more years of healing and challenge, of strengthening his friends in this new way of life was being shattered. God was recasting and purifying Jesus' vocation. Quite naturally he resisted. He struggled against his death and the end of his dream of how the kingdom of God was to be realized. Yet in the end, he recognized that the dream he had been pursuing did not belong to him, but to God. Finally he let go his plans and clung to the hope that God's dream was stronger than death.

In Jesus' death, a dream dies and a new vision begins to stir. Within this disturbing mystery of life and death, the particular dream that would in time be called Christian began to grow. The followers of Jesus slowly and painfully learned that their best dreams are, finally, not their own and that they come to life by means of death. If our vocation is not our personal possession, we are more open to let it change. The cross stands at the center of the Christian dream not out of morbidity but out of the realization that this is how we grow. Vocations and dreams rigidly adhered to become idols; ambitions too strongly defended are not Christian. Christian dreams, named for the person who most powerfully shapes our hope, must change until they better match the hope that God is dreaming for us.

As Jesus was forced to re-imagine the dream of the kingdom of God, so were his followers in subsequent generations. At certain times Christians identified the kingdom with another world, far removed from this "vale of tears." Pessimistic about changing this sorry world, Christians longed for the realization of their dreams in heaven. At other times the followers of Jesus have given a more earthly shape to their hope: God's dream of justice and peace is meant to be realized in our lives here and now. Social and political life are meant to reflect and pursue Christian values that have the power to change *this* world. This orientation to the dream of the kingdom, instead of counseling patience until the end, urges an energetic participation in changing society until God's hope for us becomes real.

The ambiguity of this dream (Can it be realized in human history or does it lie totally beyond us?) reminds us that Christian responses to this dream will range along a continuum. At one extreme stand those Christians who are convinced that the kingdom of God has nothing to do with this sinful world; we can only hope and pray for deliverance and inclusion in God's heavenly kingdom to come. At the other extreme stand those Christians who are convinced that God's kingdom must be realized in this world through some specific political party or program. The former extreme neglects the connections between social responsibility and heaven's rewards; the latter extreme too easily identifies its own dreams and agenda with God's. Between these extremes range the various and pluriform efforts of Christian communities to be faithful to this powerful dream, which is at once within our responsibility and beyond our control.

The dream of the kingdom of God does not exist only in the pages of scripture. This vision survives and thrives in lively gatherings of Christians. Our inherited hope energizes contemporary communities of faith. In their worship and their efforts for justice, in the lives of their committed members and in their welcome to outsiders, these communities display the Christian dream. In the next chapter we will consider how communities of faith keep the dream of the kingdom alive.

FOR FURTHER REFLECTION

To make this discussion of Christian dreams more concrete, consider your own dream. In a mood of reflection and calm, recall your best and deepest hope for your own life. What is this dream in your life right now? Take time to let the images and hopes and feelings emerge.

Reflect, then, on how your dream has grown and changed over the past years. How do your current hopes connect with your earlier dreams? Have elements of a previous ambition been lost or let go? What new dreams are emerging in your life these days?

Finally, think of your own hopes in the context of the kingdom of God. Select one of the gospel passages in which Jesus speaks of the kingdom of God.

Read the passage prayerfully, spending time in reflection. Then consider these questions: What connections do you sense these days between your own life and the kingdom of God? What challenge does this passage raise to your life right now? How does this the image of the kingdom of God speak to your experience of Christian community?

ADDITIONAL RESOURCES

The biblical image of the kingdom of God continues to inspire rich sources of theological and pastoral reflection. Norman Perrin examines the gospel tests in *Jesus and the Language of the Kingdom*, (Philadephia: Fortress Press, 1976). Rosemary Radford Ruether explores their social implications in *The Radical Kingdom* (Mahwah, N.J.: Paulist Press, 1975). Jon Sobrino urges a return to the image of the kingdom as crucial to an understanding of Jesus in *Christology at the Crossroads* (Maryknoll, N.Y.: Orbis Books, 1978).

In *The Kingdom of God: Challenge for Today's Christians* (Kansas City: Sheed & Ward, 1990), Cora Marie Dubitsky offers a helpful resource for use in a variety of pastoral settings; see also *Liturgy, Justice, and the Reign of God: Integrating Vision and Practice* (Mahwah, N.J.: Paulist Press, 1989), by J. Frank Henderson, Kathleen Quinn, and Stephen Larson. James W. Douglass draws parallels between our own historical situation and the setting within which Jesus proclaimed the Kingdom, in *The Nonviolent Coming of God* (Maryknoll, N.Y.: Orbis Bookss, 1991).

In *The Kingdom of God in History* (Collegeville, Minn.: Liturgical Press, 1991), Benedict T. Viviano examines religious efforts to realize the kingdom, throughout Christian history and today.

CHAPTER EIGHT

COMMUNITY AS MEDIATOR OF DREAMS

A Christian community stands at the intersection of three dreams. First, we carry *our personal hopes* to these gatherings. When we join a faith community, we bring our personal values to this group, hoping to have them nourished. In a community of faith we are introduced to *the dream of the Kingdom of God:* God's ambition for a world transformed by justice and love. Finally, our personal hopes meet God's dream in the context of a particular community, *this* gathering of Christians. When the *dream of a community* is lively, it helps us link our lives and hopes to God's dream of a world healed of its poverty, violence, and injustice. A vital community of faith invites its members to pursue a shared dream shaped by the kingdom of God.

Christian Vocation: Maturing of a Dream

To grasp the community's role in the fostering of faith, we need to recall how God ignites our hearts with hopes and dreams. A Christian vocation is not an elitist calling, but an invitation to respond to God's deepest dream for our lives. God's call is not reserved for specialists; it draws each of us to follow Christ's witness of challenge and care for the world. We sense the first stirrings of a personal dream in childhood, as we imagine ourselves as nurse or firefighter, as scientist or missionary or president of the United States. Influenced by our family and immediate environment, fragile hopes stir within us and give the first hints of our life ambition. These early dreams are easily lost or broken. Our parents may warn us that such a hope is unwarranted. Our culture may remind us that people of our gender or class or color are excluded from such a dream.

In late adolescence and early adulthood we test our dreams against reality. In our first jobs and early relationships we tentatively try out our hopes, checking them against our abilities and against the demands of the adult world. These days, much of one's twenties is likely to be taken up with this testing of the dream. We seek jobs that will give expression to our tentative ambitions; we search for groups of people who will support our still unsure hopes. Even when our life ambition finds initial expression in a satisfying career or personal commitment, many of us experience later the need to re-evaluate and purify our dream.

We can chart the psychological maturing of an adult according to the growth of a dream: its emergence (or absence) in childhood; its tentative exploration in young adulthood; its re-examination in later years. Our lives unfold, demanding choices of love and work. It is in the face of these choices that we both receive and create our vocations. As Christians, this personal journey takes place in the midst of faith communities with values and dreams of their own. Vocation is not only vision; it includes the decisions that give shape to our lives. This dream is what we most want to do with our life. This life ambition, our vocation, runs below every specific plan and job; it struggles to survive every change and detour in adult life.

Social Setting of Dreams

Personal vocations are imbedded in social contexts. Our dreams begin within our families. They are nurtured or frustrated in neighborhoods, parishes and schools, those settings where we learn what to expect from life. These places are themselves more than just a collection of individual dreams. A social setting, especially a family or a parish, can have a dream of its own. A group's special purpose, its shared ambitions and goals, can be recognized as its corporate vocation.

The family is the original arena of our dreams. Parents are busy not only with the pursuit of their own life ambitions, but with fostering their children's dreams. An inner discipline that as parents we must learn to practice is to distinguish our own hopes from the fragile, beginning dreams of our children. Parents come, sometimes slowly and painfully, to know the hard truth of Christian stewardship: in our children we are the nurturers of dreams, the guardians of vocations that we neither control nor fully understand.

But a family is more than a collection of individual vocations. A family gradually develops its own collective dream: this group of people, responding to the many invitations of God that have both brought them together and put them in tension with each other, slowly forges its own set of values and hopes. The lifestyle and decisions that give this family its uniqueness also define its dream of Christian life. Such a family dream is often fragile. The busyness of everyday life can distract us from one another; we often seem to lack the time to share our deepest hopes. And so our sense of common aspiration can be lost or at least rarely celebrated. Or a family dream can be warped, with the ambition or needs of one member serving as constraint on all the others. But a family in which a Christian dream is alive fulfills the rhetoric of our faith: the family becomes a "domestic church."

Just as a Christian family matures in the development of its dream, so too a Christian community grows as it becomes aware of its own vocation. A parish, for example, expectably builds a shared sense of Christian purpose. How does such a corporate vocation arise? In its public actions a community hands on some version of the Christian dream, whether as an exciting hope or as a withered memory. In every liturgical celebration and educational effort, a faith community announces its dream.

The religious development of the members of the community depends on this shared dream. Until recently, "religious formation" usually has referred to the initial training of vowed religious or priests. Yet formation of its members in faith is what any faith community must be about. And the vitality of the community's dream is crucial in this religious formation of all its members.

In religious formation, a faith community invites its members to join their dreams to the corporate vision of the group. The assumption here is that both the community and the individual have a dream. The balance between the individual and the corporate dream is most important. A faith community is not a neutral zone in which individuals pursue their separate vocations. Nor does a community provide vocations for individuals who would otherwise be directionless. Recognizing that the Spirit is alive in all believers, exciting them to life ambitions that contribute to the kingdom of God, a community of faith invites its members to pursue their vocations as part of the community's larger dream and purpose. Further, a community offers models of many specific ways to follow a Christian vocation. It displays—in its liturgies and program for social justice, in the lives of its talented and concerned members—the Christian dream at work. The individual is invited to let his dream, her vocation, grow within and contribute to this community's hopes.

The community's corporate vocation is also challenged and changed by individual dreams. Every vocation, and this includes each individual and each community in the church, remains in need of purification. The purification of a community's dream may begin as new dreams arise among individuals in the group. Members of a parish staff imagine new forms of collaborative ministry; board members of a Catholic hospital begin to envision more effective ways of serving the very poor; women in our communities dream dreams of priestly ministry. Such dreams are often threatening because they challenge the adequacy and stability of the group's current vision. Since it is likely to disturb our accustomed ways of experiencing our faith, we may judge a new dream to be a mere illusion, a passing enthusiasm that will soon disappear. Yet we know from our history as a religious people that new dreams have been part of the important movements of growth and renewal among us. New dreams can break open collective hopes that have become too rigid; they can challenge ambitions that have grown too safe and shortsighted. Our religious heritage has been profoundly affected by individual dreams breaking into and altering our collective sense of purpose. We think of Francis of Assisi, Catherine of Sienna, Ignatius of Loyola, Teresa of Calcutta. But this same dynamic also happens in more ordinary ways in our faith communities today. If it is confusing, it is also expectable. The collective dream of a community must support and challenge the growth of individual vocations, just as these individual dreams contribute to and, at times, challenge the community's dream. And both dreams, individual and corporate, must remain open to the enlivening critique and purification provided by God's continuing revelation of us to ourselves.

A community's dream also shares the vicissitudes and fragility of individual vocations. A group's vision grows and matures, but it can also wither and be lost. A community may abandon its dream, just as individual believers may allow their own religious hopes to die. When this happens in a parish, Sunday worship and special collections may continue, but the vision is gone. Members are exhorted rhetorically to follow the gospel, but there is no longer any excitement or ambition to transform the world in the direction of the values of Christ.

As a faith community loses its vision, personal vocations wither. In the absence of a strong sense of corporate calling, without attractive examples of the Christian dream being lived out, individuals turn to other life ambitions. As a result, Christian values of love and justice penetrate less powerfully the fabric of their daily lives.

If a community can lose its dream, it can also allow it to narrow into a rigid and compulsive vision. This happens when a community seizes one aspect of Christian life (for example, personal piety or liturgical renewal or political action) and gives it exclusive and obsessive attention. In one group, then, being "born again" becomes the only acceptable credential of Christian holiness. Another, in its enthusiasm for protecting unborn children, neglects other concerns of Christian justice and mercy. Among others, the sense that the church must "take a stand" on a politically sensitive issue closes them to the challenges or alternative insights of other Christians. Each of these dreams attempts to simplify the complex vision of Christian life. But doing so easily leads to a kind of idolatry. This partial vision is identified with God's will for everyone. A single action or conviction establishes one's orthodoxy and goodness. Antagonistic defense of "our vision" replaces a broader and more open pursuit of the elusive kingdom of God. A community's dream, like that of an individual, can become a tyranny. Like any tyranny or compulsion, such a dream is recognized by its rigidity and lack of freedom. Defending its narrowed vision of "what we must to do to be saved," it tends to neglect its own need for continual purification.

The shared dream of a parish or school or religious congregation is, thus, very much like a personal vocation. Fragile and in need of purification, the group's dream is continually being revealed to it. And like an individual vocation, a Christian community's dream is imbedded in a larger vision and hope, the dream of the kingdom of God.

Conclusion

A Christian vocation may be described as a dream, God's dream for my life, developing in my imagination. Such a dream is gradually revealed to us in the various achievements and reversals of adult life. Since it is sometimes fragile, a personal vocation may be neglected and then wither. Or it may become compulsive and too well defended. Christian ministry always entails a fostering of dreams: clarifying and purifying our vocations, we come closer to imagining what God is about in our lives.

These personal dreams are imbedded in two levels of social life. They are rooted in the immediate contexts of our families and faith communities. And these groups have their own vocations, similarly frail but exciting. Christian maturing requires the interaction of dreams: our personal hopes in dialogue and in tension with our community's dreams and goals.

Both our individual vocations and our community's dreams are imbedded in the inherited hope for the kingdom of God. This ancient dream is both the beginning and end of Christian vocations. In Abraham's dream our vocations began; our best ambitions seek to make the kingdom come true. About any individual or community vocation we may ask: "What does it have to do with the kingdom of God?" Here we find the standard against which we judge the value of our dreams.

Our vision of the kingdom of God is itself a gift of faith. Alone, we could not sustain so improbable yet compelling an image of the future. And even when we are gifted with this hope, we are always close to losing it. The evidence against this vision is staggering: how is it the blind will see? Where is the good news being preached to the poor? Who knows whether justice will prevail? Unbelievers scoff at our illusions. How are we to deal with our own doubt?

One response is to seize this ancient dream in all its ambiguity. This hope of justice and mercy is always being realized and simultaneously always being frustrated. Every act of care and reconciliation brings this shared dream closer to reality. Each act of justice and courage, private or public, enlivens the dream of the kingdom. This ancient hope is realized everyday—in us and despite us. Each "coming of the kingdom" demands celebration because our hope is so fragile. When we celebrate these actions that bring the kingdom, we are reminded of a deeper paradox: the kingdom comes through our actions but its origins are not in our power. The hope of Jews and Christians springs from a source deeper than their own good will.

If the kingdom of God is always in the process of realization, it is also and simultaneously always being frustrated. Every personal and communal act of rejecting others as unlike us, every act of violence, defeats this dream. These actions argue that the dream is nonsense, no more than a vacant, religious fantasy. Every act of an institutional church that is self-centered or defensive works against the dream of the kingdom. This ancient hope is constantly being denied, even by those who profess to carry it to the nations. If our failure as a church is a source of scandal, it also reminds us that the church is not the kingdom, but its humble servant.

Christian maturing is thus an interplay of three dreams. In the mutual jostling, critique, and support of these three dreams, we continue to uncover the purpose and possibility of our Christian life. Here too we see anew the place of the church itself. No longer sensing itself the proud possessor of God's unambiguous plan for humankind, the church guards a fragile and partial vision of God's dream for us. As a church we have yet to imagine what God has in store for us. If this humbles us as an institution, it can also excite us because we are in the midst of a revelation. All the dreams have not been dreamed; the church's vocation is still being revealed.

In his life, Jesus both proclaimed the coming of the kingdom and announced its location: "The kingdom of God is within you" (Luke 17:21). We might still ask: "Where is it within us?" The answer may be that it is in our imaginations. The dream of the kingdom of God is real because it already exists in us. It is frail and in need of nurturance because it exists mostly in our imaginations. This dream of God is not simply beyond us; if it were we could not even imagine it. It is within us, and not just in an individualistic fashion. The "you" of the New Testament statement is plural: the kingdom of God is stirring in our shared visions, in our community's ambitions and hopes. Surviving the clash of different hopes and visions, we generate in our shared life that ancient dream of the kingdom of God. Pursuing our vocations, personal and corporate, we move this dream of God closer to its realization.

This is good news for communities of faith. God's dream for human life, dreamed relentlessly for thousands of years, comes alive again in *this* group. And as this community dares to dream, takes time to listen to and clarify its own hopes, it provides the fertile, prophetic soil in which personal vocations grow.

REFLECTIVE EXERCISE

Trace the maturing of your own vocation by asking the following questions:

1. When did I first become aware of my ambition for my life? (Take time to return in your memory to explore the early shape of this dream.)

2. How have my best hopes for my life mellowed and changed over the past decade?

3. What is the most significant crisis that my dream and vocation has undergone? How was my dream threatened, or wounded, or purified in that crisis?

Then explore the connections between your personal vocation and the social dreams that influence it. Begin by identifying the dreams or deepest hopes of a group that is important in your life. This may be your family or a work group or a faith community.

4. How does this communal dream support your own vocation?

5. How do your own dreams and hopes contribute to the group's vision and sense of purpose?

ADDITIONAL RESOURCES

Thomas Rausch presents historical evidence of the continuing capacity of Christian communities to bring the gospel to their members and to the wider world in *Radical Christian Communities* (Collegeville, Minn.: Liturgical Press, 1989); see also H. Bavarel, *New Communities, New Ministries* (Maryknoll, N.Y.: Orbis Books, 1988). Jerome Neyrey examines the interplay of believing communities and the early understanding of Jesus in *Christ Is Community: The Christologies of the New Testament* (Collegeville, Minn.: Liturgical Press, 1990).

Daniel Levinson explores the role of the dream in men's development in *The Seasons of a Man's Life* (New York: Alfred A. Knopf, 1978). We develop the notion of dream as vocation in our *Seasons of Strength* (New York: Image Books/Doubleday, 1986).

CHAPTER NINE

Ministering to the Sense of the Faithful

The bishop from Michigan rose to address his colleagues. The place was Washington, D.C.; the occasion, the annual meeting of Catholic bishops gathered for discussion and decision making. Noting the painful gap between official statements and the experience of most Catholics, Bishop Kenneth Untener urged the assembly to reconsider the church's teaching on birth control. The bishop's argument rested on the practical faith of his own diocese. He reported the results of a recent conference with his diocesan council, a committed group of mature Catholics serving as his pastoral advisors. When asked their honest response to the official Catholic position, Untener reported, "Twenty-two out of twenty-three had serious questions about our teaching on birth control."

In his address, Bishop Untener appealed to the *sensus fidelium*, an ancient conviction that Christian communities possess an inner instinct of faith. This conviction attests that local churches—dioceses and parishes, justice networks and faith-sharing groups—are more than passive repositories of official teaching. These religious communities nourish the *sensus fidelium*, the sense of the faithful. As their members grow into the full adulthood of Christ, vital communities develop a reliable sense of belief, a trustworthy awareness of the demands of the gospel in their own time and place. But to mature in this way, communities must nurture an inner authority that guides their faithful action. Developing vital communities today demands a ministry to this sense of the faithful.

Instincts, Feelings, and Faith

The sense of the faithful is rooted in our religious instincts and intuitions. But instinct and intuition make many of us uneasy. The words themselves call up murky images of unconscious biological drives. Is not Christian belief a certainty that liberates us from the moods and impulses that sometimes threaten to overturn our lives? Is not religious faith that gift of personal conviction that rescues us from the tumult of feeling?

Many Christians have learned to define faith as intellectual assent, an act of the mind that does not depend on volatile and changing emotions. Others of us have been taught that moral choice is essentially a question of will power; Christians must make the difficult decisions about what they "ought to do," and not be led astray by what they "feel like doing." Often enough under this pedagogy, what starts as a healthy questioning of what our feelings mean soon leads to a general suspicion of emotional life. Feelings, now no longer our allies, are neglected or banished. And when they return, they come to punish.

The renaissance in Christian spirituality these days includes a renewed optimism about human emotion. Affection, anger, consolation, confusion, joy—these are expressions of the human spirit. We are more aware today that feelings are part of the life of the Spirit as well. With re-awakened respect for these powerful resources, Christians today are trying to understand better how emotions are a part of the journey of faith.

Contemporary spirituality gives increasing attention to discernment, the process by which we come to wise decisions in the important questions in our life. Is it time to leave this job? Should we have another child? What does justice demand of us here? What direction should my priesthood take now? Questions like this always require a response before all the facts are in. We decide, often with trepidation, guided by intuition and by a gradually more confident "sense" of how we are to act. Discernment depends on the education of desire, a gradual process that refines our feelings and renders our instincts trustworthy. Our hunches become wise in repeated purification; they may even become holy.

Christian liturgical life nurtures this purification. Here our emotions are shaped by prayer and gesture, by music and memory. Thus shaped, they can guide and enhance our celebration of God's presence among us. Liturgy is a school of the senses. In worship we recall Jesus' delight and anger and sorrow. We remember and celebrate his sense of when to confront others, when to heal, when to retreat. And the ritual movement of the liturgy is meant to shape us as well, forming our feelings so that they may display something of the power and nuance of Jesus' emotions.

Gospel Feelings

In the New Testament the Greek word *phronein* carries several suggestive meanings: sensible, cunning, wise. The parable of the ten young women (Matthew 25:1-13) distinguishes between the five who were foolish and the five who were sensible *(phronein)* enough to bring extra oil for their lamps. Being sensible here means knowing what to do, having the good instincts that lead to effective action. In Luke's gospel (16:1-8) we find a surprising story: a dishonest steward, about to be fired for his misconduct, makes friends with his employers' debtors by reducing their obligations. At the time of his dismissal, the employer praises the culprit for his *astuteness.* Here *phronein* describes a clever instinct to make the best of a bad situation. *Phronein* appears again in the account of Jesus commissioning his disciples. He sends them on their mission with the advice "to be *cunning* as serpents and yet as harmless as doves" (Matthew: 10:16). Sensible, astute, cunning: *phronein* names the practical wisdom that enables us to respond appropriately to challenging situations.

An even more instructive use of this word occurs in the story of the disciples' reaction to Jesus' decision to go to Jerusalem (Matthew 16; Mark 8). Jesus has determined that he must go to the capital to confront the authorities. Although he knows the danger involved, Jesus senses it is time to act. Peter objects to this plan and strongly argues his case. Here two strong-willed men clearly feel differently about what is to be done. Suddenly angered, Jesus utters one of his most emphatic statements: "Get behind me, Satan. You are an obstacle in my path, because you do not *sense* (phronein) the things of God, but those of humans" (Matthew 16:23). Peter's instinctive response—to avoid Jerusalem and its dangers—is opposed to "sensing things the way God does." Peter's response seems sensible to him, but Jesus finds its blameworthy. Peter has followed his instincts, but the wrong ones. In going to Jerusalem, Jesus follows other instincts, a sense of how he is to act that has been formed by his attentiveness to his Father.

Many readers miss this crucial discussion of opposing instincts. Most English translations disguise or drop the emotional connotations of *phronein* in favor of more cognitive renditions. The Jerusalem Bible, for example, has Jesus say "The way you *think* is not God's way, but man's." In the Oxford Revised Standard translation, all sensing disappears in "You are not on the side of God, but of men."

In Paul's first letter to the Corinthians (13:11) we come upon another use of *phronein*. Describing religious maturity, Paul turns to the metaphor of human development: "When I was a child, I used to talk like a child, *feel (phronein)* like a child and argue like a child, but now that I am a man, all childish ways are put behind me."

Again we encounter an opposition of ways of behaving, rooted in ways of feeling. Religious maturity demands we let go our childish ways, transforming our feelings so that they become more trustworthy resources. But again the nuance of feeling is lost in most translations; both the Jerusalem Bible and the Oxford Revised Standard translate this passage as "to *think* as a child."

Paul's most emphatic statements about Christian feelings appear in his letter to the Romans. In chapter eight, he makes the famous distinction between those who live according to the flesh and those who live according to the Spirit (8:5). The first group sets its heart on (*phronein*) the things of the flesh, while the other sets its heart on the things of the Spirit. Here again, most English versions render the phrase as "set their minds on." A more faithful translation would be "are attuned to." *Phronein* is a practical wisdom by which we become attuned to the rhythms of God's Spirit.

Seasoning of Instincts

How do we attain this practical wisdom? How does a community's sense of faith mature? To understand the communal process, we must examine this transformation in our personal lives.

We are each of us gifted with a range of powerful feelings: delight, anger, affection, grief. As we begin the journey of faith, our instincts and inclinations are already being shaped by our surroundings. As anthropologist Claude Levi-Strauss observed, human instincts are never "raw;" they are always "cooked," shaped by our culture and influenced by our environment. Our ways of reacting, whether in rage or sorrow or affection, are never simply spontaneous. These are carefully, even if often unconsciously, learned from life around us. The values and biases of family and neighborhood and society form our feelings.

The image of *seasoning* helps capture the process by which our feelings and instincts mature. Growing up in a Christian family and participating in a parish community, gradually we learn how Christians respond. We watch how those whom we cherish act. We observe how Christians treat their own bodies, how they are present to those whom they love. We sense over many seasons how Christians respond to "others": the poor, the sexually marginal, those who speak other languages and display different cultural habits. Over years of practice, we pick up how Christians celebrate God's presence: the kind of events that bring us together, how our minds and hearts and bodies are to be brought into worship.

Christian maturing is this seasoning of instincts. In conscious and more subtle ways, our feelings are gradually formed by Christian values and hopes. Communities of faith provide both the context and the examples for this formation. And, of course, as with every human effort, we often fail at this formation. A family displays its distrust of the body; a parish congregation communicates its suspicion of sexuality. A religious tradition is used to justify outright rejection of "others," who are judged to be excluded from God's family. We must acknowledge how these negative dynamics, too, have formed the instincts of those who call themselves Christian. Communities of faith today are challenged to be places where these wounded feelings can be both confronted and transformed.

Several nuances enrich the image of *seasoning.* First, the metaphor points to a seasoning agent, an external influence that promotes the maturing process. The life of Jesus, present to us in word and worship and mutual witness, seasons the community and its sense of faith. Second, seasoning suggests considerable duration: forming our feelings according to Christian hopes for justice and charity takes time. Only gradually and with expectable reversals do we become seasoned Christians.

Third, being seasoned suggests both *familiar with* and *good at.* Seasoned veterans have a lot of savvy; they know instinctively, often without complex consideration or arduous argument, how to respond. As seasoned Christians, we are steeped in the values of Jesus Christ. Gospel ideals are no longer merely external norms. Now internalized and personalized, these values shape our lives. Our responses, once so subject to external influence and our own shifting moods, become more reliable. Mature Christians are those whose instincts—who is our neighbor, when to seek reconciliation, how to protest injustice—can be trusted. This process of being seasoned is ongoing in our lives, for we have never fully and finally "put on Christ." But in this process, our instincts become more dependable. No longer simply alien or unpredictable, our feelings gradually become our friends. Their inner authority now helps guide our actions.

Such is the special fruit of Christian adulthood. With these inner resources to rely on, we are less susceptible to the cultural seductions of consumerism, competition, conformity. In Paul's words, "Then we shall not be children any longer, tossed one way and another and carried along by every wind of doctrine, at the mercy of all the tricks people play and their cleverness in practicing deceit" (Ephesians 4:14). Though we sometimes fail and fool ourselves, we can more habitually and more thoroughly trust the movements of our heart. Thus purified and matured, we are readied for that most important exercise of Christian adulthood: handing on to the next generation the practical wisdom of how Christians believe and act.

A Community's Sense of Faith

A Christian community is both a location and an agent of religious maturing for its members. But how does the community's sense of faith itself mature? God's Spirit dwells within each genuine community of faith. This indwelling shapes the moods and influences the movements of a group of believers. As the group develops and is purified under the Spirit, a maturing "sense" of its faith supports and guides its decisions as a community. *Lumen Gentium,* the document on the nature of the church developed in the Second Vatican Council, underscores the vitality of this shared religious sensibility (para. 12, our emphasis): "It *clings* without fail to the faith once delivered to the Saints (see Jude 3), *penetrates* it more deeply by accurate insights and *applies* it more thoroughly to life."

If *clinging* suggests stability and continuity, *penetrating* and *applying* point to development and change. A lively sense of faith, then, involves more than a docile attitude toward what has been received; it requires an active and constructuve instinct that deepens and develops as a community applies its faith "more thoroughly to life."

Exploring this active sense of a community's faith in his book, *The Modern Theology of Tradition*, J.P. Mackey quotes German theologian Scheeben (p. 121, our emphasis):

> The profession of faith by the body of believers is not of value only by reason of the influence of the Magisterium, which begets it, but possesses *its own intrinsic, relatively autonomous value* as a result of the direct working of the Holy Spirit on the faithful.

A community's sense of faith is not simply passively received from authoritative leaders. This instinct, generated by the Spirit of God, is intrinsic to the group itself, rooted in its maturing faith.

A century ago, John Henry Newman turned to this notion of the sense of the faithful to argue for the importance of the laity in the preservation and growth of Christian faith. A prominent theologian of Cardinal Newman's time had argued that Christian revelation is given first to the hierarchy and only then handed on to faith communities. In a treatise entitled *On Consulting the Faithful in Matterns of Doctrine*, Newman took issue with that understanding. He insisted that Christian faith abides and thrives in actual communities; it does not pre-exist in a privileged way in the hierarchy. Indeed, Newman continued, the development of dogma comes about from the official church's reflection on beliefs already long present in vital communities of believers.

Newman defined the sense of the faithful "as a sort of instinct or *phronema*, deep in the bosom of the mystical body." This religious instinct may be experienced, Newman says, "as an answer to its (the community's) prayer." Newman seems to be pointing here to the gradual development of the sense of faith, a sense experienced less as a perennial understanding than as a deepening insight on the journey of faith. In our own time, for example, Christians come together in many places to explore the complex issues of abortion and euthanasia, of economic justice and ecological responsibility, of personal ethics and systemic sin. They pray for a deeper awareness of the faith dimensions of these vexing questions. Their prayers will be answered as these deepening insights gradually coalesce into a seasoned wisdom to guide the community in its faithful action.

Ministering to a Community's Sense of Faith

We come in touch with the practical sense of faith that energizes a community by exploring its religious identity: "Who are we, and what are we to do?" A group's instincts of faith are rooted in its shared history. What we have learned on the journey—how we celebrate God's presence, how we can care best for the next generation, how we are to seek justice in a complex world—gives shape to our common vocation. These lively forces awaken us from an inappropriate dependency on distant authorities and remind us that the Spirit is active in our midst.

Ministry to the sense of the faithful begins here, in an awareness that this body of believers *has* such a sense. This ministry matures in efforts both to strengthen and to purify the community's seasoned instincts. The group's experience of faith, a gift of the Spirit, may also be wounded by bias and sin. Every vital religious community, then, embraces the challenge of continuing purification, to penetrate its faith experience more deeply and to apply these convictions more thoroughly in its life.

Giving attention to its own sense of faith draws a religious group to reflect on its relation to the larger church. A maturing community recognizes the mutuality that links it to the church universal. Our local gathering is grateful heir of the larger tradition; from this generative source we have learned to follow Christ. The wider church and its official leaders remain our essential companions in faith, guiding us on the journey and calling us to the disciplines of communion. But the local community is accountable as well to its own growing sense of faith. This wisdom, developed slowly and sometimes painfully, is part of the community's gift to the larger church.

For Catholics, especially, this mutuality is challenging. Conventionally, we pictured the church hierarchically, with religious wisdom descending from the pope and bishops to local communities and believers. Obedience ascended from these local settings to authorities "higher up" in the religious organization. But a lively sense of the faithful draws us to another image of the church: a community of sisters and brothers in the Lord, rather than a hierarchy of superiors and inferiors.

In a religious world of mutuality, leaders not only ask obedience but practice it themselves. The root of the New Testament word for obedience, *akouein*, means "to listen to." Leaders must pay attention to the sense of faith maturing within the groups for whom they care. The gospel sense of *akouein* survives in the word "acoustics." Religious leaders obey by seeing to the acoustics of a community. They serve obediently by nurturing a climate open to the subtle movements of the Spirit. Obedient leaders confront the animosities and stagnation that ruin the acoustics in a faith community. Obedient leaders help the groups in their care bring their seasoned experience to the larger church, even when this risks disagreement and conflict.

The sense of the faithful testifies to God's unfailing presence among us. We cannot isolate this promised presence in any one group or limit it to a single historical time. God moves at will; our obedience is to listen to the compelling invitations of the Spirit, wherever these are heard. Obedience requires patience, as a community's sense of faith develops and is purified. Obedience requires the courage to bring a community's convictions to the larger church and the seasoned flexibility to survive the controversy that is sure to follow.

REFLECTIVE EXERCISE

The sense of the faithful is a sign of the religious vitality of a community. To help this understanding become more concrete, consider a faith community that is important to you—a parish group, an intentional community, a ministry team. Then reflect on these questions.

1. How do members participate in the community's decisions and actions. Be concrete; give examples.

2. In what areas of its life does this community characteristically trust its own resources, have confidence in its own sense of direction? In what areas does it characteristically look "outside" for direction or approval?

3. What questions—concerning worship, ministry, justice, sexuality, education, authority—are being discussed or debated in the community now? How successful is the group in dealing with its own diversity? In moving toward consensus? Has the community been able to express its sense of faith concerning one of these significant issues?

ADDITIONAL RESOURCES

Bishop Kenneth Untener's address appears in *Origins,* November 29, 1990; the quotation is from p. 405. The complete text of the Document on the Church *(Lumen Gentium)* is available in *The Documents of Vatican II,* edited by Walter M. Abbott and Herbert Vorgrimier (New York: Crossroad, 1989).

Cardinal Newman's intriguing reflection on the sense of the faithful can be found in *On Consulting the Faithful in Matters of Doctrine* (Kansas City: Sheed & Ward, 1961, 1989). J.P. Mackey examines the sense of the faithful in *The Modern Theology of Tradition* (New York: Herder & Herder, 1963); the quote from Scheeben is on p. 121.

Mary Benet McKinney provides a practical design for drawing on a community's sense of faith in the process of group decision making in *Sharing Wisdom* (Allen, Tex.: Tabor, 1987). Robert J. Schreiter discusses the importance of the community's experience to the development of theology in *Constructing Local Theologies* (Maryknoll, N.Y.: Orbis Books, 1985). In *Sharing Faith: A Comprehensive Approach to Religious Education and Pastoral Ministry* (HarperSanFrancisco, 1991), Thomas Groome develops a useful model for pastoral reflection to guide a group's efforts to discern its practical sense of faith.

For a fuller discussion of the dynamic of obedience in the adult community, see Ch. 16 "Obeying as Partners," in our *The Promise of Partnership: Leadership and Ministry in an Adult Church* (HarperSanFrancisco, 1991). We have explored the role of the community in theological reflection in *Method in Ministry* (San Francisco: Harper & Row, 1980); see also James D. Whitehead, "The Practical Play of Theology," in *Formation and Reflection: The Promise of Practical Theology* (Philadelphia: Fortress Press, 1987), edited by Lewis Mudge and James Poling.

PART THREE

PARTICIPATING IN THE COMMUNITY OF FAITH

CHAPTER TEN

The Leader's Task

The Catholic experience of leadership has undergone significant transformation over the past quarter century. Over this same time, the way that leadership is understood in the social sciences has shifted dramatically. How do designated leaders contribute to a community's life? What is the relationship between the leader's style and the group's vitality? Based on a broader appreciation of what goes on in groups, we come up with new answers to these questions. This chapter offers a developmental model of how groups grow and examines ways that leaders help—or hold back—this process.

Group life is dynamic. Communities grow and change. The possibility that there is a pattern in these changes intrigues many people. Social psychologist Roy Lacoursiere, for example, looked at studies tracing the development of small groups. He found that these investigations reveal a common pattern of change as groups matured. Lacoursiere identified this sequence, found repeated in groups of many different kinds, as the stages in the life cycle of groups.

The term "stages" strikes many people as too deterministic, suggesting a schedule that every group necessarily follows. So some analysts speak instead of common phases of group experience or expectable shifts in group focus. But, even with this caution about terminology, most investigators recognize a pattern in how groups grow. The best image, perhaps, is one of shifting priorities: at different moments in a group's development, different questions come to center stage, demanding members' time and attention.

Pattern of Group Development

Four recurring themes shape a group's development. These are inclusion, power, intimacy, and effectiveness. While these dynamics play throughout the group's life, not all are equally "live issues" all the time. At different moments in a group's history, different issues assume critical importance. The differences are not simply random; a pattern is involved. For example, questions of "Who belongs?" precede questions of "What can we accomplish together?" But the sequence is expectable not inevitable, since so many factors influence what goes on in groups.

Inclusion

As a group gets started, "who belongs" is an issue. Inclusion means belonging, becoming part of this group. Potential members ask: Do I want to belong to this group? How can I become involved in its life? What will it mean for me to be a member? To answer these questions, we may look within ourselves to determine how we feel about the group. Or we may look to others for assurances that the group accepts and appreciates us. Inclusion raises questions of the group's identity, too. What is this group all about? Are its goals worthwhile? Is membership here worth the trouble?

These questions of identity absorb the attention of a group just forming. Inclusion issues can also arise later in a group's life, at any point of crisis or significant change: in membership, in leadership, in purpose. When a group undergoes these changes, members often experience a loss of cohesion. We are caught up again in the issues of "Who belongs?" "Who are we now as a group?"

Power

A second priority in the group's life is power. The group's task now is to learn ways to share influence and control. Questions arise: Does this group welcome our gifts? Will we be able to help shape what goes on here? For our group to grow, we have to find ways to put our different strengths at the service of the group's goals. In some groups, members confront their concerns about power openly by discussing their expectations and negotiating their roles. Taking up these questions of power marks a new level of group maturity. Developing common understandings of authority, decision making, and dissent, we craft this group's power structure and find our place in it.

In other groups, the power questions erupt in a power struggle. Members attack each other or blame the leader or turn against the group as a whole. But even in this more conflicted setting, people's goals remain the same: to establish and test the group's pattern of power and to find their place in it.

When power issues come to the fore, groups experience considerable strain. Sometimes members become openly hostile. Even without this disruptive behavior, we often face anxiety, misunderstanding, and blame. While seldom pleasant, these negative emotions are a necessary part of a group's development. Indeed, our conflict over power issues indicates that we are genuinely engaged in this group. The struggle signals that a new level of group commitment is possible. However, for conflict to lead our group to this new level of maturity, we will need to handle it well, and this may be difficult. But we must see the issues of power and conflict for what they are—not simply and automatically a sign that our group is in trouble but rather an indication that we are approaching a new phase of group life.

Intimacy

Working out how we will deal with one another raises questions of closeness. In most groups, these intimacy concerns arise only after we face the earlier power issues. Now we ask: How close do we want to be in this group? What can members confidently expect of one another? How safe is it here to admit our needs?

A wide range of possible responses to these questions of closeness exists. No one level of intimacy fits every group. Some groups develop strong networks of emotional support among members. Other groups tend toward "cooler" patterns which keep emotional sharing at a minimum. Neither trend is, of itself, better or more mature. The optimal level of emotional intimacy depends on group composition, norms, and goals. As our group establishes the pattern of relating that works for us, we have to negotiate these questions of emotional closeness. The process of working out this pattern is ongoing, but at times in our group's life these issues of "who are we for one another" come into special focus. Here, as in the power issues, the very question disconcerts us. For some, to focus on what is going on among us signals that the group has gotten off track: "We are here to do a job; it's a waste of time to be talking so much about ourselves and each other." Others of us are embarrassed to admit that we want or need anything from other people. Because of our hesitancies, attempts to discuss what is going on among us in the group often provoke resistance. Dealing with this interpersonal agenda demands sensitivity and persistence. For all the awkwardness this discussion generates, here again, as when power conflicts arise, the strain often indicates that a new stage of group maturity is now possible.

Effectiveness

The new stage comes as members consciously turn their resources to the group's tasks. To be sure, many groups are task groups by definition; as these groups start, members have a job to do together. But early on, even in formal task groups, issues of inclusion, power and closeness preoccupy many people. As we struggle together to resolve these earlier questions, members become more committed to the group and its work.

Now, questions of effectiveness focus our attention on the group's goals. How do we marshal our diverse talents and energy for the shared tasks that confront us? As individuals, we ask: What can we accomplish with this group that goes beyond what we can do on our own?

At this point, the group's challenge is to nurture its chief asset—the talent and commitment of the members—and to manage these resources well. Effective patterns of decision making, practical strategies to keep our motivation high, workable lines of coordination and evaluation—these organizational concerns become key. Group participation expands, as members encourage one another and share the work. As a result, group satisfaction increases. As we discover that both our work and our relationships thrive, the tension between people issues and task issues fades.

This productive season in the group's life carries its own kind of distress. Since the demands of the task can be considerable, the group's resources may well be strained. But morale is high. We sense that we are getting back from the group at least as much as we give. The rewards of membership amply compensate us for any stress we may experience.

But this phase of high effectiveness does not last indefinitely. Changing external circumstances, internal group fatigue, or a host of other factors can interrupt the group's momentum. Earlier group issues often return to center stage, upsetting our sense of priorities. Questions of inclusion, or power, or intimacy come to the fore. Sometimes this shift is a truly a regressive move, taking us back to a set of earlier, probably unresolved, issues in the group's life. More often, though, the re-emergence of these issues invites us to move forward. These old questions—now asked anew—generate fresh responses, reflecting the group's new level of maturity.

Leadership in Group Development

As these critical issues emerge and the group's internal priorities shift, leadership patterns change. At different stages in our group's life, we make different demands of our designated leaders. Some of our expectations are appropriate; by meeting these, leaders help groups move to higher levels of functioning. Other demands we make of our leaders are less healthy. The response of the designated leader to these shifting demands helps determine whether a group stagnates or moves forward.

Inclusion

At the beginning of a group's formation, our sense of the group's power is minimal. No "us" exists that members can count on, so we seek answers and assurances elsewhere. So, often we look to the person designated as leader for the personal recognition and approval we need. In addition, we want the formal leader to provide answers to the question "Who are we as a group?" Since we sense that the leader *should* have answers, we interpret any confusion or ambiguity over the group's purposes (very normal in a group at this stage) as the leader's fault. If our group has as yet no formal leader, we cast in this role one of our members whom we sense to be powerful according to some outside criteria. Thus, we often look to a man before a woman, a priest or religious before a layperson, a professional before a working-class person, someone with credentials before a volunteer. If the designated leader cannot or will not help us deal with the group's early issues of inclusion and identity, we become angry and frustrated. This frustration sometimes turns members away from the designated leader, forcing us to look elsewhere for the reassurances we need. Often, though, the group simply disbands.

Some groups at this stage pressure the leader to function as a dominant, even parental, figure. A dominant leader can serve the group's development here by providing structures that help us clarify our expectations and by modeling behavior that shows us how to work together. But early dominant leadership draws us to expect that the person in charge is responsible for meeting the group's needs. We fall victim to the illusion that the group's power resides primarily in this designated leader. Over time, our demands on the leader increase dramatically, as does our confusion. The group's needs for answers, for assurances, for a sense of direction overwhelm the leader. Initially leaders feel consumed by these demands, then gradually resentful of the dependence of the group and, finally, alienated from the "needy" followers who seem only to take and to give nothing in return.

Designated leaders who continue this dominant posture too long risk fostering paternalism. Among themselves, group members become bitter. A leadership style that allayed our anxiety in the early stages of our group's formation now fosters frustration. Once we establish the pattern that only the leader can meet our needs, then our dissatisfaction grows even as our sense of personal power declines. Formerly, our dependence on the leader made us feel secure; now this bond only reinforces a lingering sense of inadequacy.

Power

This tension around dependence brings power issues to the fore. When concerns about power arise, the group's patterns of leadership fall under attack. A member or a small group questions some established way of doing things. If the formal leader responds to this as a personal challenge, the battle is joined. Other members feel pressured to take sides; sometime we unite in a shaky coalition against the leader.

The distress here signals a process of power redistribution underway. Members are begining to recognize the group's over-dependence on the leader. The leader's dominance, once acceptable and even preferred, now seems insulting. As the group grows stronger, we sense the power discrepancy that exists between the leader and the rest of us. To remedy the now unacceptable arrangement, we attempt to re-define the leader as "just one of us"; that failing, we try to force the leader out.

Redistributing power does not come easy; dismantling our familiar patterns risks conflict and confusion. Some groups respond with counterdependence, refusing to acknowledge any power differences as legitimate: "We are all equals here; no one is more in charge than anyone else!" Or we substitute one dependency for another, putting "our choice" into the designated leader's slot but leaving our expectations of dominant leadership intact. But since the dynamics of power have not changed, "our choice" soon becomes "the enemy" and the battle continues.

To exit this vicious cycle we need to focus on the patterns of leadership, not on the leader. We must reinterpret where power exists and how power functions among us. The designated leader is part of a larger interplay of influence and initiative that makes our group strong. Resolving the leadership crisis means recognizing this give-and-take of power and, in this light, redefining the leader's role.

The designated leader can be more than a "victim" of this process. The way that the leader responds to the initial power challenge significantly influences the group's move beyond dependence. When we first question leadership, the leader occupies a position of considerable power. If the leader uses that power against the member who questions, the rest of us learn that new patterns of influence will be hard won. The leader here demonstrates that the stakes are high in the process of growth. The designated leader who does not respond as if under personal attack teaches a different lesson. We learn that power is not a possession to be jealously guarded but a resource that can be examined, accounted for, and even shared among us.

Intimacy

When questions of closeness are of greatest significance among us, the role of the designated leader becomes crucial in another way. Sometimes the intimacy issue focuses on the person of the leader. We see the leader as the one who should satisfy our interpersonal needs. Each of us seeks a special relationship with the leader. We view this relationship as more satisfying than any that we members might develop among ourselves. In fact, developing bonds with one another is downplayed or even discouraged. In groups like this, our commitment to the leader is unclouded by competing emotional allegiances. But loyalty to the leader alone frustrates the group's growth toward greater cohesion and effectiveness.

Our group matures to the degree that we develop satisfying ways to give and receive from one another, not just from the leader. When members feel connected with the group only through their intense relationship with the leader, groups suffers. The behavior of the designated leader is important here. Personable leaders help groups thrive. But leaders who need to be the exclusive focus of affection stymie group development; instead, we dissipate our energies in the volatile struggles of love and hate, favoritism and jealousy, allegiance and disloyalty.

On the other hand, leaders nurture groups by encouraging mutual support and assisting us to develop these bonds among ourselves. Effective leaders introduce structures to foster interaction, both work procedures that foster cooperation and social opportunities for informal times together.

Effectiveness

When a group matures to this stage, our sense of resourcefulness and participation is high: "We can do it, and each of us has something to contribute." Clear objectives and effective behavior become our priorities. Leaders contribute by supporting the procedures and strengthening the interactions that make us effective.

To work together effectively as a group, we need to sharpen our understanding of the common goal, commit our individual resources to the shared effort, and coordinate our activities to achieve the best result. Groups at this stage look to leaders to keep this larger vision alive and to keep their activities on track. However, neither the vision nor the task belongs solely to the leader. The designated leader functions at this stage as custodian of our vision and facilitator of our task.

But not all groups reach this mature understanding. Many groups are tempted to treat the leader as the one who is "really" in charge. If we have not resolved the issues of group identity, power, and intimacy, facing our external task with a sense of competence and confidence is difficult. We then see the designated leader as the only one who knows what should be done and how to go about doing it. Since the task is "really" the leader's, our commitment is minimal. The designated leader in this kind of group can feel abandoned in the work: "No one else seems to care; no one else feels responsible; I have to do it all myself. What do I need a group for anyway?" The leader feels that doing the work alone is easier than trying to involve this passive and resistant group.

Effective leaders know that their central role is not, on their own, to *accomplish* the group's work (though, like the rest of us, leaders often have particular talents or skills to contribute) but to *assure* that the work is done. As groups mature, control and coordination responsibilities tend to be shared among group members rather than left as the leader's sole responsibility. Patterns of shared information and decision making develop, along with expectations of collaborative action and mutual accountability.

A group at this stage risks concentrating exclusively on the rational aspects of their goal-directed activities. We take the demands of our work seriously; we set achievement goals; we may even develop a healthy competition as we invest time and energy in the group's tasks. Leaders introduce strategies of problem solving and monitor the group's productivity, to help us accomplish what we set out to do. Sometimes these goal-directed efforts absorb the group's attention, casting the leader as a task figure and leaving our interaction with one another focused on achievement.

When this happens, we overlook other aspects of our life together. During periods of high productivity, the more-than-rational dynamics of shared life suffer. But group commitment is most deeply nourished at this extrarational level. For our group to remain vital, we must tend to these elements of cohesion and commitment, of symbol and celebration. These dynamics nurture a group's shared dream, calling forth our commitment to loyalties that go beyond the task at hand.

Leaders must be alert to this level of a group's life. In some groups (and this is especially true in religious groups), we view the designated leader as the person most directly responsible for nurturing us at these deeper levels. Thus, a religious group suffers if the leader does not—or cannot—respond to our extrarational needs. But here again, the designated leader is not the only one who can meet our need for symbol and celebration. Other members, too, have imagination and talent to enhance the extrarational life of the members. The designated leader's role is often to call out these talents in others, thus supporting the group's activities of ritual and play. Without these, we may well exhaust ourselves in our tasks and lose the savor of our group's deeper sense of purpose.

FOR FURTHER REFLECTION

Bring to mind a community that is important to you, recalling the people involved in the group and your history together. Think now of a recent experience of the group acting at its best, functioning well as it pursued a project or faced a crisis or accomplished a goal.

List for yourself the responses that went into the group's success: suggestions made, actions taken, obstacles overcome, conflicts resolved.

Now consider the role of the group's designated leader(s) in this example. How did the formal leader contribute to the community's success? Be concrete; give practical examples.

Where there ways in which this designated leader hindered the group or limited its effectiveness? If so, how? Again, offer concrete examples.

What insight or learning about the leader's task do you take away from this reflection?

ADDITIONAL RESOURCES

In *Leadership Ministry in Community* (Collegeville, Minn.: Liturgical Press, 1987), edited by Michael Cowan, the contributors discuss historical, theological, and sociological factors that shape leadership in the community of faith. Letty M. Russell examines leadership in *Household of Freedom: Authority in Feminist Theology* (Philadelphia: Westminster, 1987).

Rosine Hammet and Loughlan Sofield look at leadership at different stages of group life in *Inside Christian Community* (New York: LeJacq Publishers, 1981). Henri Nouwen takes up a spirituality of leadership in *In the Name of Jesus: Reflections on Christian Leadership* (New York: Crossroad, 1989).

Helen Astin and Carole Leland provide a provocative look at alternative models of leadership, based on the experience of key women involved in social change, in *Women of Influence, Women of Vision* (San Francisco: Jossey-Bass, 1991). In *That They Might Live: Power, Empowerment and Leadership in the Church* (New York: Crossroad, 1991), Michael Downey draws together a range of contributors to discuss the foundations of leadership in the religious community. For an excellent statement of his now-classic account of power as relational, see Bernard M. Loomer, "Two Conceptions of Power," *Process Studies*, 6/1 (1976), pp. 5-32.

In *The Life Cycle of Groups* (New York: Human Sciences Press, 1980), Roy Lacoursiere presents a summary statement of research findings treating the "stages" in group interaction. In *Paradoxes of Group Life* (San Francisco: Jossey-Bass, 1987), Kenwyn K. Smith and David N. Berg explore the inevitable internal tensions that accompany group maturing. Hedley G. Demock focuses his discussion on leaders working in human service settings in *Groups: Leadership and Group Development* (San Diego: University Associates, 1987). Joseph Rost examines and expands James McGregor Burns's influential understanding of the leader's role in *Leadership for the Twenty-First Century* (New York: Praeger, 1991).

James Bacik offers a helpful analysis of the connections between religious leadership and theological reflection in *The Challenge of Pastoral Leadership: Putting Theology into Practice* (Cincinnati: St. Anthony Messenger Audiotapes, 1990). Patricia Gundry examines the challenges faced by women in leadership roles in *Neither Slave nor Free: Helping Women Answer the Call to Church Leadership* (San Francisco: Harper & Row, 1988). For a fuller discussion of our own understanding of the ministry of religious leadership, see *The Promise of Partnership: Leadership and Ministry in an Adult Church* (HarperSanFrancisco, 1991).

CHAPTER ELEVEN

Now You Are the Body of Christ

Michael A. Cowan

Two forms of small community life are part of the Christian community movement in the United States today. One might be characterized as mainstream, the other as marginal. Mainstream communities usually develop as part of parish life, often having the revitalization of the local congregation as an explicit goal. The marginal communities more often arise out of dissatisfaction with parish experience, even alienation from denominational life. These communities, often ecumenical in membership, frequently have an uneasy relationship with formal religious institutions. The mainstream and marginal forms of small community life have much in common, but their differences in motivation and practice should not be ignored. In the foreword to this volume, Art Baranowski describes the significant work he is doing with parish-based small communities. My own discussion of beginning and sustaining a small community of faith is focused on the experience of marginal communities.

The members of our house church gathered initially as middle-class

Michael A. Cowan is associate professor of practical theology in the Institute for Ministry, Loyola University, New Orleans. He is married and the father of three daughters. He and his family are members of a small community of faith in New Orleans which is actively building partnerships with other small communities and participating in a city-wide community-organizing effort. He is co-author (with Bernard Lee) of *Dangerous Memories: House Churches and Our American Story*.

religious consumers. Basically we were individuals who sensed in varying ways that the models of economic and professional success held out by our culture did not add up to the good life. Grabbing for all the gusto we could get, exploring in therapy the intricacies of our personal histories and our marriages, even "owning a piece of the rock" had left us with a nagging sense of emptiness. While the advertising media promised that "it doesn't get any better than this," our own experience told us otherwise. So we came together at the start as part of a spiritual search, looking for something more for ourselves and for our families.

We were an ecumenical group, composed of nine adults from the Roman Catholic and Reformed traditions, along with our children—of which there were thirteen, ranging in age from two to twenty. As we began, some members carried unresolved bitterness and resentment toward their religious heritage. Others had basically positive memories of their religious upbringing. Most of us were somewhere in between. In our own lives and as heads of families, everyone in the group had struggled with questions of religious observance. Alternative traditions—feminism, ecology, Native American culture, Eastern religions, existentialism—held interest for many people. How could we nurture a common spirituality?

Family Gatherings

After fairly intense initial discussions, we determined—somewhat ambivalently—to start with the symbols and texts with which we were most familiar. Christian Scripture, then, became the focus of our gatherings. At the outset we met as families every other Sunday for about two hours, followed by a communal meal. These meetings took place on a rotating basis in the homes of the five families in the community. Gradually a pattern evolved for this time together.

1. A time for greeting of one another and welcome by the host family, ending in a song.
2. A reading of a scriptural text from a children's Bible by one of the children.
3. Twenty minutes spent with our children in three age-related groups, on activities developing the theme of the biblical text.
4. Table ritual led by the adult hosts. Our usual pattern included opening song, remembrances of people and intentions, community

prayer, sharing of bread and cup, greeting of peace, and closing song.

5. At this point, our children left us and the adults turned to a period of scriptural reflection. In this adult liturgy of the word, we used a four-step reflection process. We began by allowing time for members to respond freely to the reading from their own perspective. Next, we turned to an exegesis of the passage, to help us hear the text on its own terms. Then we spent time together in dialogue with the text and about the text. Finally, we tried to identify the practical "differences for our life" that came as the fruit of our communal encounter with the Word.

Rather than completing this reflection in one meeting, our practice was to return to the same text over four successive gatherings. Originally we adopted this approach for pragmatic reasons: our children's presence usually limited this "adults only" time to thirty minutes (if we were lucky!). We soon recognized that this practical strategy brought unexpected benefits. Returning to the same scriptural passage over a period of some weeks gave us time to build up a sense of familiarity with the text, to explore its meaning, and to let it question our lives. This disciplined approach had a surprisingly powerful impact on the members of our community, many of whom had never read the classic biblical texts both appreciatively and critically as adults.

6. A shared meal to which each household contributed a dish, followed by informal conversation and a community cleanup. This final informal time together extended from one to two hours, depending on the commitments of the host family and other community members.

From the start, members in our community felt comfortable in the focused discussion and in the informal time we shared. Developing rituals of prayer in common proved more challenging. Over three years together, however, a style of shared prayer emerged that was authentic to the community's experience and formative in our lives beyond the group. Two factors critical to the spiritual depth of our prayer gatherings were the care we gave to the selection of the music and the effects that carried over from our sustained encounter with Scripture.

Expanding the Adult Sharing

After about six months together, several members expressed the need for another kind of conversation, uninterrupted by the expectable demands of our children's presence at the family gatherings. We needed more time together as adults, sharing the rigors and joys of forging a style of living less dominated by the fierce materialism and individualism of our culture. So we determined to gather as an adult community every other Saturday evening. Our purpose was to take up some of the questions of personal and communal concern that required discussion in greater depth.

Over the months that followed we considered a range of themes. Some issues were general in scope: contemporary forms of spirituality, faith development in adulthood, self-esteem and dependency, relationships between women and men. Others were more personally immediate: facing the hurts and resentments we carry from our past, clarifying a critical career decision, confronting the influence of consumerism and materialism in our own lifes, nurturing the spiritual development of our children. A wonderful sense of informality and spontaneity—of relaxation and play and companionship—characterized these adult gatherings, enriching our time together as families.

Thus the commmunity gathered, alternately as families and as an adult group, for most of the weeks of the year. For busy and successful people in this culture, our community's constancy was itself an accomplishment! In addition to these regular meetings, we planned special community gatherings during the Christmas and Easter seasons and scheduled periodic adult retreats. Community participation was strongest from September through May; sustaining regular meetings was most difficult over the summer months, June through August.

This faith community proved to be an important setting for marking critical times in our families. In addition to the frequent delight of commemorating birthdays, we celebrated together the birth of a child, the deaths of the fathers of three group members, the departure from home of one family's first child, a divorce, and a family's leaving the community as part of a job relocation. In the United States, such marker events tend to be experienced privately or within the limited context of the nuclear family. As a result, many of us feel isolated at such critical times and these significant experiences lose their authentic public character.

Shared among us, the personal events of birth, death, divorce, and moving away have taken on greater significance. As a community, we have experienced their sacramental character. For example, my wife prepared a ritual of farewell for our daughter who was leaving for college. This community ritual touched every parent and child present, influencing not just how we will say goodbye when the time comes but how we hope to be together in the meantime.

Confronting Our Marginality

Individuals in our group had differing relationships with various denominations, ranging from continuing alienation through weekly participation to recognized leadership roles. But as a community we found our place at the margins of church structures. This marginality left us free within the community to raise our questions and doubts authentically and to wrestle vigorously with each other about them. And anonymity was not a problem among us; we experienced Scripture and ritual in the context of a loving and supportive group in which we were known personally.

Our marginality had a negative side. As a small group, we were responsible for everything that happened or failed to happen among us. We did not have the challenge and support—the anchoring—to which we would have access in a community located more fully within a larger institutional body. The metaphor of anchoring is particularly apt to our experience. All of us need the anchor of traditions which support a sense of continuity and of relationships which nurture our identity. Yet none of us wants to be *anchored down* by these connections, limited in inappropriate or self-destructive ways. How do we find a creative balance?

After about two years had passed, we began to discuss very tentatively the possibility of affiliating as a group with a local church. Earlier, this prospect would have been impossible for us to consider. Even now, how the issue will be resolved remains unclear. But raising the question invites us to reexamine our marginality, perhaps to move toward the center, perhaps not.

Pursuing Our Public Life

Social involvement has been the most difficult issue faced by our community. In this, I believe, we are similar to most middle-class faith communities in this country. Community is impossible without a significant degree of mutual care among members. But to claim the name of community of faith, without a significant communal engagement in the public world, is equally impossible. A biblically-attuned small community will never be comfortable with being just a support group.

Small communities of faith have a public face as well as a private life. This issue of our public commitment consistently provoked tension and misgivings within our community.

Our ongoing encounter with Scripture repeatedly raised the question of our involvement with the surrounding world. After much honest and difficult discussion, we took up a commitment to periodic service in a local Catholic Worker community. Despite some wonderful personal, family, and communal moments, we were unable to sustain this group commitment past its early phase. This failure is a sign, I think, of our group's unresolved ambivalence toward questions crucial for all faith communities: Is it necessary to respond *as a community* to the issues of justice and peace-making that we encounter in our shared reading of Scripture? Or do our *individual* commitments adequately discharge the obligations with which those texts face us?

My own reflection is that as a small community facing situations of political and economic injustice, we were no less subject to paralysis than is an individual facing those challenges. If anything, we were in greater jeopardy because we *had* to return regularly to these issues! Our commitment to shared Scripture reflection subverted our individual tendencies to denial or numbness. Praying together rubbed the wound raw.

Taking up our cross in this world—our neighborhoods, our cities, our nation, our planet—is not primarily a private matter of being better individuals, although of course we have this responsibility. Nor is meeting the gospel's challenge simply a matter of gathering with others to share our faith and to support one another personally, although no authentic community is imaginable without such fellowship. Genuine Christian community also requires that we face together the true state of our social body—our public world.

When small Christian communities take up our cross and follow Jesus, we will inevitably be led into the public arena. This is the realm where sexism, racism, and political and economic injustice are perpetuated and must be confronted. A small faith community that does not find itself in this public arena has lost its way. The culture of individualism and consumerism offers us endless inducements to go astray in an addictive pursuit of material possessions and endless self-actualization. It is precisely in the public world that communities of disciples must be prepared to lose our lives in order to find them. In all societies, Christian people on the margins—the "people of the base"—understand this readily and find there great hope. But this is a hard saying for small communities in the middle-class culture of a highly individualistic society.

Alone, individuals and isolated intentional communities cannot face events in the public arena with any measure of hope. Even communities which face these forces in solidarity with others must expect moments of crucifixion. But our Christian heritage witnesses to the remarkable conviction that crucifixion is not the last word; that there is a new form of shared life that arises not after death but out of it; that the experience of Good Friday—and *only* that experience—gives way to Easter.

If we read the scriptural texts on justice and the cross alone—whether as individuals or isolated faith communities—they will simply break our hearts. A larger solidarity is required of us if we are to be challenged but not demoralized by their powerful demands. Let me share one direction in which this larger solidarity can be pursued. At present I am part of an experiment to join networks of small communities of faith with others in broad-based community organizations committed to social transformation. These organizations, involving inter-racial and inter-faith alliances, create a new and sustainable base of citizen power for change. The Industrial Areas Foundation has pioneered this approach to community organization, which now flourishes in settings from East Brooklyn to San Antonio to Los Angeles. In the judgment of many observers, these broad-based coalitions are changing the ways in which political and economic business is conducted. The wedding of small Christian communities and these community organizations holds promise of a creative resurgence of public life in faith communities in the United States.

Practical Guidelines

I close with these practical suggestions for beginning and sustaining small communities of faith.

1. What community means for a group is learned by living it, not by agreeing in advance to certain abstract principles or processes. So don't wait for theological agreement on all major issues, or for the resolution of all personal ambivalence about religious issues, or for the reform of the sexism or racism of the institutional church before you begin an experiment in small community life.

2. To put this point more positively: spend some time developing a working consensus of what is expected together—and then start. Be prepared to listen respectfully to the questions and discomforts that subsequently arise in the group, as well as to the joy and healing which happen. Community is not a state in which we begin but an accomplishment that emerges from shared and sustained commitment.

3. Since bonding as a community takes time, getting started slowly is wise. Meeting regularly is more important than seeing how quickly members can move to deep levels of sharing. In that spirit, early in the group's experience leave plenty of time for members to share stories of their spiritual search and to name the life concerns that are genuinely important to them. Having infomal time together is important throughout a group's life and never more so than in the beginning.

4. Sustaining a community's life with fewer than ten adult members is difficult, since time demands and schedule complications frequently lead to the absence of one or more members at community gatherings. A group of more than fifteen adult members will have difficulty establishing and sustaining the level of self-disclosure and trust that a small faith community requires.

5. A profound way to nurture a small community of faith is to gather regularly to encounter Scripture in a way that releases its power for our daily lives. The format we found helpful allows the free expression of initial reactions to a text, provides sufficient exigetical and historical background to make the text intelligible in its own right, encourages candid expression of member's positive and negative responses to the message of the text, and invites them to imagine the future in light of this encounter with the Word.

Theologian David Tracy reminds us that scriptural texts have the provocative power of religious classics. People in this culture, as people everywhere, entertain religious questions—though they are more likely to call these concerns "spiritual questions" or "questions of meaning." When these questions meet scriptural texts in a climate of genuine mutuality, when this conversation extends over a period of time, lives change. Hunger grows for gathering regularly with other searchers around these texts. This is the hunger that both leads to and sustains an intentional faith community or house church.

6. From their beginnings, small communities need to read with Scripture in one hand and the newspaper in the other. The texts of

Jewish and Christian Scripture were written as responses of faith communities to the concrete historical worlds in which these groups found themselves. The texts need to be read today in relation to such a world, not merely as private spiritual resources. A sustained and shared reading of Scripture and society will press a faith community beyond its internal concerns to come to terms with its public mission.

If questions of the faith community's public face are left to emerge "naturally" at some later date, the community may be unable to transcend a sense of itself as a support group. Its public mission must be discerned (and re-discerned) from the outset. This ongoing discernment process thrives when the group functions in solidarity with other faith communities, citizen organizations, and the larger church.

7. The special challenge of leadership within small communities is keeping the proper balance between management and mutuality, in a social setting in which relationships are as important as the tasks to be undertaken. Leaders within intentional communities must tend that difficult balance competently and faithfully.

The only model of leadership appropriate to the small community of faith, indeed, the only appropriate model for the Christian exercise of power and authority, is the leadership of mutual service. Leadership within intentional faith communities is primarily a matter of facilitating a collaborative, democratic process among community members. In such a process, many voices must be given a hearing, differences acknowledged, common interests identified within inevitable diversity, and courses of action taken which genuinely reflect a consensus of concerns among those involved. The hallmark of authentic communal leadership is the capacity to promote a unity which is respectful of the diversity of gifts present among us.

The qualities of servant leadership are not mysterious or magical. Authentic leaders invite participation. They acknowledge the contributions of others. Willing to share their own views—including their questions and doubts—they learn to challenge respectfully and hold themselves open to challenge. In the face of diversity, they seek creative consensus as the way for the group to go forward.

8. The interaction of women and men stands as a great divisive issue in Christian communities today. One side of the issue is interpersonal: it has to do with the unconscious distortion of face-to-face relations between men and women due to unresolved issues from our personal

histories. The other side of the issue is institutional: it has to do with the systematic exclusion of women from full participation in the structures of religious institutions. I am convinced that the small community of faith is a significant context of mutual healing in our interpersonal relations as women and men. In addition, these faith groupings are potent settings of mutual empowerment for men and women committed to confronting the institutional structures of gender discrimination.

9. Over time, the experience of authentic Christian community inevitably places us in tension—even confrontation—with the dominant culture. Given our profoundly individualized culture today, it is perhaps inevitable that the tension emerges first in the question: "How can I fit one more activity, one more commitment, into my life?" Soon, however, we find ourselves asking another question: "To what in my culture must I say 'No!' so that community has room to flourish in my life and that of my family?" For many of us, then, joining as communities of faith has shown us the way to personal liberation. As more and more of us recognize today, these communities hold within them the seeds of social and cultural transformation as well.

FOR FURTHER REFLECTION

Look back over the nine practical guidelines (pp. 119-122) that Michael Cowan lists from his own experience as a participant in a small faith community. Consider how these insights about small intentional communities fit your own experience in the community of faith, whether in a base community or a parish or other setting.

1. Which of Cowan's convictions are closest to your own experience of participating in a faith community? Give some examples.

2. Do any of Cowan's guidelines seem at odds with your experience? Again, offer concrete examples.

3. Are there ways in which Cowan's comments challenge your own community of faith? How is this so?

ADDITIONAL RESOURCES

Robert and Julia Banks explore faith communities as a way of being church in *The Home Church: Regrouping the People of God for Community and Mission* (Sydney: Albatross Books, 1986). In "Households of Faith in the Coming Church," *Worship* 57/8 (1983), pp. 237-255, David Power offers a compelling analysis of the emergence of small groups of Christians in non-traditional ecclesial structures. Vincent P. Branick studies Paul's instructions to the earliest communities of faith in *The House Church in the Writings of Paul* (Collegeville, Minn.: Liturgical Press, 1989).

For fuller description of the work of the Industrial Areas Foundation, see Harry Boyte, *Commonwealth: A Return to Citizen Politics* (New York: Free Press, 1989) and Mary Beth Rogers, *Cold Anger: A Story of Faith and Power Politics* (Denton, Tex.: Univ. of North Texas Press, 1990). In *Biblical Integrity and People Power* (Chicago: Institute of the Church in Urban Industrial Society), William Ramsden and John Montgomery reflect on the theology that emerges from the community organization experience; see also William Droel and Michael Slattery, *Christians in Their Neighborhood* (Chicago: ACTA Publications, 1990).

Michael True invites families and communities to identify the connections between their ordinary lives and the issues that confront the world in *Ordinary People: Family Life and Global Values* (Maryknoll, N.Y.: Orbis Books, 1990). In *Catholic Worker Houses* (Kansas City: Sheed & Ward, 1990) Sheila Durkin Dierks and Patricia Powers Ladley discuss the Catholic Worker Movement and the communal commitment of those who take up this ministry of service and witness.

Mary Sue Taylor provides practical resources for developing rituals in faith communities in *Traveling Together: Prayer for Gatherings* (Cincinnati: St. Anthony Messenger Press, 1992). For a thoughtful reflection on the vital role ritual plays in a group's life, see Tom F. Driver, *The Magic of Ritual* (HarperSanFrancisco, 1991).

CHAPTER TWELVE

Personal Resources
for Intimacy

Community brings people together in ways that can change us. Participating in a community, then, requires resources of both mind and heart. Psychologists describe these strengths as resources of intimacy. As used here, "intimacy" is more than a synonym for sexual experience or romantic love. Intimacy refers to the resources we have for being close to other people. We tap these qualities whenever mutuality come into play: in friendship, family life, work collaboration, community involvement. Our strengths of intimacy help us welcome the exhiliration and tolerate the strain that come with close relationships.

To situate intimacy in a broader context, one that goes beyond sexuality and romance, consider a crisis that may arise when we try to collaborate. For example, we volunteer as a member of a task group at work, at school, in our church, or in the neighborhood. As the work progresses, we start to feel uncomfortable: No one person is dominating the group or impeding its work, but still we feel somehow crowded. What other people do affects our work. Our own plans do not always prevail. Suggestions we make look different after other members have dealt with them. We feel that things are not going as they should, as we expected they would. Two impulses are at war within us: to gain greater control of the situation ("If only they would do things my way!"), or simply to withdraw ("Clearly, this group does not appreciate what I have to offer; I'd be better off acting on my own."). In a mood of increasing discomfort and disorientation, we vacillate. But what threatens us here? We are afraid others may overwhelm us, absorbing our identity as well as our ideas.

This example parallels our ambiguous experience of drawing close to someone as a friendship develops. The differences are obvious but the dynamics are the same. As the relationship deepens we hesitate, afraid that in drawing close we might lose ourself. We are tempted both to flee and to control. But the hope of finding a better way to be close helps us face our fear.

These examples put us in touch with an underlying dynamic in community. Most of us experience a normal, expectable tension when we draw close to others, whether in work or in friendship. Very basic concerns generate our stress: If I let these other people influence me, what will become of my sense of myself? If I come close to you, will I survive? Will my idea survive, if I share it with this group? Will my plan survive, if I bring it up in this committee? Will my identity, my self-esteem, survive this close encounter?

These questions greet us at the threshold of intimacy: Are we sure enough of ourself to risk being close to other people? Are we comfortable enough with who we are to let someone else really know us? Are we sufficiently confident of our own ability to risk being influenced by others? When we participate in community, we will face these questions again and again.

Every community asks its members to share some significant part of their lives. The dialogue that is appropriate in a particular community —the religious education faculty of a diocesan high school, for example—may not link us in deep personal friendship, but it will require openness and self-disclosure. To function as a community, we must give others access to some important parts of ourself: our values, talents, ideas. Such openness leaves us vulnerable, exposing this part of our identity to confirmation, to challenge, to change.

Participating in community, then, involves a willingness to be influenced. This encounter carries the risk of an altered sense of self. When we are unsure of who we are, this risk seems too great. Close contact with other people threatens us: "Will they see through me? Will I be found out? Will I be hurt?" To protect ourself, we develop a defensive interpersonal style that keeps others at a distance and leaves little room for mutuality.

Community and Friendship

Relationships in community hold so much promise. The hope of mutual support attracts us. We yearn to find here a deeper level of communication than we know in the rest of our lives, one that can bridge the barriers that often separate us from one another. In looking to a community for these benefits, our hopes are not misplaced. As intermediate styles of group life, communities encourage members to share each other's worlds to a greater degree than do most of the organizations and task-oriented groups to which we belong. But sometimes our hopes for community are translated in images of close friendship. Confusion begins here. Deep friendship and devoted love are crucial in personal development; on this, both personal experience and the findings of psychological research concur. Close friendship and community sometimes overlap, when the special bonds of deep mutuality develop between people who belong to the same group. But to take close friendship as the goal of a community's life or as the sign of its success is risky.

Friendship and community are two different kinds of relationship. Recognizing this difference does not suggest that genuine intimacy has no place in a community's life. In fact, intimacy is a key resource for community. Participating in a community both tests and strengthens our capacity for closeness. We expect, and appropriately so, that interaction among us in a community will go beyond the limited and role-specific relationships we know elsewhere. We want more from community. This "more" involves greater availability to one another, a real engagement in which mutuality plays an indispensable part. We expect the giving and receiving to go both ways. This interplay may take place at many different levels. We may share our work, our religious values, our common commitment to social reform. In a community, both our ideas and our emotions are engaged, both what we do and who we are. For most of us, however, these experiences of communal intimacy differ from the special interdependence of close friendship.

Cooperation and Competition

Very often, as we have seen, the term "intimacy" refers to experiences of friendship and love. This makes sense, since we learn intimacy's most important lessons in experiences of close friendship and mutual love. But adult intimacy takes us beyond these special relationships. For many people, experiences of cooperation and competition are significant settings of intimacy. Whether in work or play, cooperation and competition test our self-awareness, our self-assurance, our empathy with others, and our capacity for interdependence. Cooperation involves us in joint action to accomplish a common goal. Competition puts us in opposition to one another as we pursue goals that are important to us both. Both competition and cooperation are expectable in community groups, since both are normal dynamics in ongoing relationships.

Some examples may help us see how cooperation and competition connect with intimacy. For instance, we need the resources of intimacy in a meeting of the parish committee charged with planning the annual fund-raising supper. Success in this event is crucial to the parish budget; without the proceeds of the supper, we would have to double the tuition in the parish school and cut back our contribution to our sister parish in the inner city. To cooperate in this committee, we must each be aware of the particular contribution we can make to our common goal, a contribution that necessarily reflects both our strengths and our limitations. We must be secure enough with these strengths to offer them to the group task, even with the risk that our offer may be rejected. We must be flexible enough to accept that others may modify our suggestions or challenge our ideas. We must be empathic enough to take pride in what we have accomplished together, just as in other situations we rejoice in what we accomplish on our own.

Without these resources, cooperating fully will be difficult for us. Consider this example. At the parish meeting, Gregory volunteers to coordinate the plans for moving people in and out of the dining area. This job is central to the financial success of the fund-raiser: a bottleneck in the dining room means long lines, disgruntled parishioners, fewer meals served. But, as most parishioners know, Gregory is quite disorganized. He is warm and gregarious and fun to be with, but he has a hard time making plans in advance or anticipating problems. Serving on a welcoming committee or acting as master of ceremonies for the social program that follows, Greg could make a great contribution to the success of the parish supper. But he would make a poor dining-room coordinator. While his offer to supervise the dining area may express good will, it does not indicate that Gregory knows how to cooperate. In this instance at least, he lacks the self-awareness that is necessary for effective cooperation; he is unclear about his own contribution to the group's goal.

Both self-awareness and self-confidence are essential for cooperation. We must be able to offer our help, to put forth our idea, to sketch out our plan without waiting to be coaxed. Most of us can recall a situation where we were not confident enough to be very cooperative. We held back a suggestion, afraid that it would strike others as farfetched or foolish. We were reluctant to volunteer ("suppose they really don't want me on their committee!") and waited to be asked. Obviously, this reluctance is sometimes appropriate, but needing to be coaxed makes cooperation difficult.

To be able to cooperate well also requires personal flexibility. Working together means that our ideas and plans are brought "up close" to others. Expectably, this contact affects us. We may find that we agree from the start; then the interaction simply confirms and reinforces our original stance. But our interaction may have a different result; we question one another's ideas, modify each other's plans, invite one another to see things differently. The disagreement may disquiet us, putting us on the defensive. Or we may experience this challenge as an opportunity for clarification and growth. Personal flexibility like this comes from an appreciation that both change and compromise can express our integrity.

Most of us value the ability to cooperate, aware of its advantages to ourself and others. But competition carries a bad reputation. Many therapists, educators, and religious persons share the conviction that competition should be eliminated. This conviction is born of their experience with competition's negative effects. But competition also has a positive side. An ability to compete maturely is an important ingredient of adult personality. And the psychological characteristics of the mature competitor are remarkably similar to those of the mature cooperator. For example, to compete well in sports, we must have a realistic sense of our own abilities, with an awareness of both our strong and weak points.

But to compete as well as to cooperate, we need more than self-awareness. We must know our game, but then we must also play it. Competition forces us to test our ability against a concrete challenge, with the risk that we may not prevail. (If we play only the games that we are sure we will win, we are not likely to be considered a good competitor!) To compete is to take a chance, to accept a risk. When we compete, we play with the realization that in any one instance our current level of strength or skill may not be sufficient. But only by accepting the risk of failure can we confirm and develop our strengths.

Finally, the exchange of competiton reveals much about each participant. In the contest, we come to a better knowledge of ourself and to a special awareness of our opponent. Our success in the game is often dependent upon flexibility and creativity in modifying ourself in response to what we learn about our rival.

These characteristics (awareness of self and the other person, a sense of self open to the demand of mutuality and to the possibility of failure, a flexible response to the individuality of other perple) are of value in more than sports. These abilities strengthen us for communal behavior— team work, conflict resolution, negotiation, planning. They are resources of intimacy often lacking in persons who cannot, or do not, compete.

We mature as a range of psychological strengths and a repertoire of resourceful behaviors become available to us. Competent adults know how to cooperate and to compete; they learn to discern when, and in what combination, each action is appropriate.

Psychological Resources of Community

Participating in community, we come into more confident possession of our own resources for intimacy. These resources are both the source and the fruit of strong communities. They find expression in the following ways:

1. a sense of self that balances a basic awareness of who we are with some openness to new information;

2. an awareness of other people that includes the capacity to see things from their point of view;

3. a willingness to be influenced by this awareness, to modify ourself in response to new information and different interpersonal situations.

4. the flexibility to incorporate personal change in ways that strengthen rather than diminish us.

5. the patience to tolerate the inevitable strain of personal accomodation and compromise.

These resources support effective communities, helping us develop patterns of behavior and lifestyle that are mutually enhancing.

Psychologist Erik Erikson describes intimacy as "the capacity to commit oneself to concrete affiliations and partnerships and to develop the ethical strength to abide by such commitments, even though they may call for significant sacrifice and compromise." Intimacy is, then, a capacity, an ability, an abiding competence of adult maturity. This strength enables us to commit ourself, not to humanity in general or to idealized movements, but to particular persons in concrete relationships. We draw on the resources of intimacy in living out these commitments, even as we recognize the limitation and incompleteness involved in our relationships.

Community relationships are dynamic. People change and relationships develop over time. Some developments bring fulfillment; others make demands for accommodation, for understanding, for tolerance, for forgiveness. A well-developed capacity for intimacy helps us sustain the adjustments and compromises of communal life, without jeopardizing our own integrity. A flexible identity, an empathic awareness of others, and an openness to continued development make creative commitment possible. These strengths support caring communities.

FOR FURTHER REFLECTION

Consider your own resources for intimacy. To begin, bring to mind the relationships that are important in your life these days—relationships with friends and loved ones, with coworkers and colleagues, in community or neighborhood or church. Then focus on one of these relationships. Recall a recent time of significance in this relationship, perhaps a time of special closeness, or a time of tension and conflict, or a time of accomplishing something together. Spend some time with the details of this special experience: the people, the events, the feelings, the outcome. Then turn to these questions.

1. What does this experience tell you about your strengths for intimacy, about the resources you bring to your close relationships?

2. What does this experience say about your frustrations in being close to people, about the limits you feel in intimacy?

3. Does this experience hold clues of how you might improve your

ways of being with other people, ways in which your personal resources for intimacy can be strengthened?

ADDITIONAL RESOURCES

Erik Erikson discusses his now-classic understanding of intimacy as a psychological resource in *The Life Cycle Completed: A Review* (New York: W.W. Norton, 1982); see also the analysis and examples in *Vital Involvement in Old Age* (New York: W.W. Norton, 1986), by Erik Erikson, Joan Erikson, and Helen Kivnick. We expand our own discussion of intimacy as a social resource in *A Sense of Sexuality: Christian Love and Intimacy* (New York: Doubleday, 1990); see especially Ch. 4, "Intimacy and Commitment," and the several chapters of Part Three, "The Arenas of Intimacy."

Dick Westley discusses the transformative power of genuine mutuality in *Redemptive Intimacy* (Mystic, Conn.: Twenty-Third Publications, 1981). Roberto Unger explores the struggle for intimacy and community, in the face of social tendencies toward domination and depersonalization, in *Passion: An Essay on Personality* (New York: Free Press, 1984).

For sensitive considerations of the tensions between women and men in close relationships, see Lillian Rubin, *Intimate Strangers: Men and Women Together* (New York: Harper & Row, 1984) and Fran Ferder and John Heagle, *Partnership: Women and Men in Ministry* (Notre Dame, Ind.: Ave Maria Press, 1989).

CHAPTER THIRTEEN

RECOGNIZING DIFFERENT LEVELS OF MUTUALITY

Michael A. Cowan

The sense of community, of belonging to groups that respond to us as individuals worthy of dignity and respect, is rooted in the experience of mutuality. Mutuality refers to the ability of persons to engage in direct and non-manipulative dialogue, each understanding and respecting the other's frame of reference. Relationships based on mutuality are lateral rather than vertical; they resemble friendship more than psychotherapy. When relationships among members of a group are characterized by mutuality, community is a genuine possibility. Mutuality within a community occurs at several levels. The differences in these levels depend on several factors: the goals of the group, the values members hold regarding personal sharing, even the operating rules that guide members' behavior toward one another. Critical to the experience of mutuality at any level will be the members' level of interpersonal skills.

Self-Disclosure and Empathy

The first level of mutuality is characterized by two related behaviors: self-disclosure and empathy. Self-disclosure means the ability to share directly with another my feelings, thoughts, and values; empathy means the ability to hear accurately the thoughts, feelings, and values from another's frame of reference.

A relationship displays first-level mutuality when the people involved share their points of view, confident that they will be heard. This stance does not imply constant agreement. Rather, the norm is that each person listens and can expect to be listened to, even when people disagree. First and foremost, people pay attention to one another. Evaluation and decision are not necessarily secondary, but they are subsequent. Empathy and disclosure at this level are concrete ways in which people offer one another support.

Just as this first level of mutuality does not necessarily imply agreement, neither does it necessarily imply emotional closeness. In many groups, our communication is more about a common work than about our personal lives. If we are to work together on a project, it is important that I can communicate directly to you my ideas, my feelings of enthusiasm or hesitation for the plan, my suggestions for changes and improvements. For us to collaborate effectively here, it is important that you can see things from my point of view, not so that you can unquestioningly adopt my proposals, but so that you can more accurately assess their potential contribution. If we are unable to communicate directly with one another about the task, this lack of basic mutuality is likely to make our collaboration more difficult.

This first level of mutuality may be thought of as the minimal requirement for basic decency in human relationships. It provides a foundation for constructive communication in all social settings—family, classroom, religious community, or work place. A group that is not characterized by such basic patterns of good communication undermines rather than supports the psychological well-being of its members, by forcing them to defend themselves in their dealings with one another.

Empathy and disclosure are the foundation on which the succeeding levels of mutuality depend. The absence of these skills makes it difficult for groups to move toward deeper experiences of community.

Challenge and Self-Examination

The dynamic interplay of support and challenge leads to the development of individuals and groups. If communities are to function developmentally, their communication must go beyond basic mutuality to include the possibility of responsible challenge. This challenge is characteristic of an intermediate level of mutuality. An essential form of healthy challenge involves the ability to invite another person to look constructively at issues, problems, or crises from a different frame of reference. The reciprocal behavior of this level of mutuality is self-examination. Self-examination depends on my willingness to receive the challenge as an invitation—an opportunity to look at myself or my position on an issue in a new light and to examine the possible validity of this alternative perspective.

Some examples may help to clarify the constructive interpersonal challenge that marks this second level of mutuality. Several members of a ministry team are concerned about another member's increasingly busy and harried work schedule. They have three basic options. They may ignore the behavior, or vent their feelings of irritation as they demand that the member behave differently, or they may confront the person directly and responsibly. In another case, a principal becomes aware that racist or sexist attitudes are interfering with the effective performance of an otherwise competent teacher. The options here parallel those of the ministry team: the leader may ignore the behavior; he or she may criticize the teacher and demand new behavior; or the teacher may be confronted directly and responsibly.

The limitations of the first response—ignoring the problem—are apparent. The individual loses an opportunity to receive information that may serve as the basis of positive change. The setting suffers as well, since necessary tasks are not carried out or are carried out inadequately. The second option—to demand new behavior—is essentially a power tactic. It may elicit temporary compliance, but ultimately it leads to resistance and defensiveness on the part of the person challenged this way. Moreover, this type of challenge is often experienced as an attack; it is likely to solidify the individual's position rather than to encourage self-examination and change. It may also complicate later communication, cluttering a relationship with negative emotions and issues that remain unresolved.

The third option—direct and responsible challenge—characterizes the second level of mutuality. It is important that such challenge be accompanied by empathy; as I confront another person I must communicate my awareness of and respect for her or his point of view. Confrontation needs to be understood and experienced by people as an *invitation* to examine some aspect of their behavior. When it is experienced as an invitation rather than an attack, my challenge is more likely to lead to exploration rather than to self-defense. Not feeling under attack, people have less need to excuse or explain away their behavior. Responsible challenge enables people to look at themselves in a new way, to examine their behavior in light of new information.

Not all relationships move to this second level of mutuality. In some settings, that makes sense. But relationships that are not open to responsible challenge are likely to remain limited and in some sense superficial. There is no development without adequate challenge. This holds true for groups as well as for individuals. Groups in which relationships operate consistently at the first level of mutuality function well, but such groups are incomplete as developmental resources. Our personal and social development is enhanced when others are direct and responsible in sharing with us different ways of looking at things, and when we respond to these alternate perspectives with a willingness to examine ourselves and to change.

Immediacy and Exploration of the Relationship

The second level of mutuality has an external focus. I invite you to examine your behavior, not as it directly affects me or our relationship but as it affects a larger value or task or goal. The third level of mutuality has more limited scope. Here we focus on our relationship itself. Immediacy is the ability of individuals to share directly with one another information about ways their behavior injures the relationship or gets in the way of collaboration. To be an effective expression of mutuality, this immediacy must be complemented by willingness to explore our relationship here and now.

The minister who experiences loneliness and resentment at being placed on a pedestal by the congregation, a teenager who feels that her own judgment is continually called into question by inflexible family regulations, an African-American supervisor who is afraid to comment on a white manager's insensitivity to potentially explosive racial issues, a lay woman on the parish staff who feels some of the pastor's expectations are demeaning—all these are examples of immediacy concerns. Facing such issues directly and positively creates the potential for opening new areas of growth in communities. Refusing to face them or facing them incompletely has the power to block that growth.

Immediacy issues are potentially powerful sources of developmental change because of their highly personal nature. These issues raise core concerns of how I am experienced in a relationship, not merely my roles, tasks, or skills—but my *self*. Our ongoing development as persons is the result of events in the network of relationships that form the context of our lives. This fact gives foundation to the statement that mutuality in interpersonal relationships is critical to the maturing of persons and communities. Obviously, the depth and intensity of mutuality differs in different groups. The intimacy of committed personal relationships is inappropriate in typical business relationships, but important interpersonal issues do arise and must be addressed even in such settings. No group—family, work team, parish, intentional community—can be fully effective if members cannot deal with one another appropriately at each of the three levels of mutuality discussed here.

Factors Influencing Mutuality

If people are to involve themselves in relationships of mutuality, five interrelated factors must come into play: self-esteem, working knowledge, skills, values, and rules appropriate to the setting. The absence of any one of these factors compromises mutuality.

1. Self-esteem People with a very negative image of self are unlikely to risk the exposure and vulnerability that come with mutuality. While they may desire to move closer, the instinct for self-protection is likely to block their efforts at intimacy. The lack of self-esteem in adult life may be related to problems of psychological development. When this is the case, psychological counseling can help. On the other hand, self-esteem can be low because a person lacks basic interpersonal skills. In this instance, effective interpersonal skills training can lead to enhanced self-esteem.

2. Working knowledge Any information that helps me to behave competently in pursuing my goals can be termed working knowledge. Working knowledge of mutuality is information that helps me to understand the behaviors and attitudes involved. For example, psychological research suggests that empathy, a basic characteristic of first-level mutuality, has two distinct components: discrimination and communication. Discrimination refers to perceiving accurately what other people are saying and how they feel; communication means letting the other person know that I have heard accurately. Without *both* components, empathy is not present. This information becomes working knowledge when it helps me to understand empathy in my own life, when it influences my behavior.

3. Skills A skill may be defined as a specific behavior or set of behaviors that can be engaged in by a person at will in the appropriate context. While working knowledge refers to what we know, skills refer to what we can do. I may, for example, understand (working knowledge) the discrimination-communication distinction mentioned above. It does not automatically follow, however, that I will be able to discriminate accurately the feelings and content of other people's conversation (skill) or communicate to them that I have understood (skill). Over the last twenty years, much attention has been given to specifying those behaviors that foster effective communication. Training programs in communication and other helping behaviors now exist, programs that can help people develop the skills associated with each level of mutuality. See Chapter 14 for more on these skills.

4. Values A value is a chosen belief that actually influences behavior. Members of a community may not establish genuinely mutual relations, even when they seem to have the self-esteem, knowledge and skills to do so. In this case, it is possible that the people do not view mutuality as an active value. They may speak of mutuality or mention it in a mission statement. But if there is no evidence of mutuality in their behavior, it does not actually function as a value. An early step in any effort to strengthen mutuality in a community, then, must be a clarification of whether mutuality is a shared value, one in which members are willing to invest time and effort.

5. Setting norms The final factor that affects the quality of mutuality in a community focuses not on individuals but on the rules and norms of the group. A religious house or seminary with a long history of interpersonal distance—the avoidance of intimacy—may find that these traditions stand in the way of establishing relationships of mutuality. A group with a strong commitment to work—serving others—may feel that time community members spend together takes away from what is really important. Norms like this interfere with the development of mutuality. A community that hopes to expand its life to all three levels of mutuality must give attention to the norms and customs that guide members' behavior toward one another.

In attempting to describe the basic structures of mutuality, my approach here has a "how to" flavor about it. I have discussed practical ways in which we can assess the extent to which mutuality characterizes our dealings with one another and offered some concrete steps to give mutuality a larger place in community life. It seems appropriate to end my comments in a consideration of the "why" of mutuality—why should a Christian community involve itself with these concerns?

My own response to this question takes the form of a brief set of propositions regarding the connections between the presence of mutuality and the possibility of personal and spiritual growth.

Every act of authentic self-disclosure
makes one life a gift to the becoming of another.

Every act of accurate empathic understanding
enhances the listener's spirit.

Every act of responsible challenge in the spirit of
empathy is an invitation to an increase in stature.

Every act of non-defensive exploration in response
to challenge reflects a commitment to a life of larger
dimensions.

Anyone who struggles to develop the tenderness, discipline, and resilience of spirit that such giving and receiving demand knows first-hand both the moments of dying and the intensity of living that can result. To care for one another and to accept one another's care in this spirit of deep mutuality is to place our ordinary acts of face-to-face interaction within the ultimate context of love.

FOR FURTHER REFLECTION

Consider these levels of mutuality in your own experience of community life. Select a particular group and dwell for a few moments in your memories of this community over the last year or so.

1. Find examples of events or exchanges that represent first-level mutuality: self-disclosure and empathy. What factors or circumstances helped this level of mutuality develop in the group?

2. Look for examples of second-level mutuality: responsible challenge and self-examination. As you see it, what might be done to support these expressions of mutuality?

3. Have you experienced third-level mutuality here: immediacy and exploration of the relationship? Are there factors that help community members to reach this level of mutuality? Are there factors that stand in the way of this level of mutuality in this community?

CHAPTER FOURTEEN

COMMUNICATION AND CONFLICT IN COMMUNITY

Community draws us close to one another. But being close to others, whether in friendship or community living or collaborative work, is not always easy. Good attitudes about closeness and cooperation are not enough. We have to translate these attitudes into practical behavior. In the give and take of our interaction, we must develop ways of being together and working together that are mutually satisfying.

Skills of Community

Over the past three decades, psychologists and other social scientists have systematically studied what happens in face-to-face communication between people. As a result, we are more aware today of what helps and what frustrates understanding in close relationships. Once we have identified the behaviors of effective communication, we can learn these graceful ways to give and receive the gift of ourselves that is at the core of community. The interpersonal skills that are especially important for community living include empathy, personal disclosure, and confrontation.

Empathy enables us to understand another person from within that person's frame of reference. Empathy begins in an attitude of openness. This enables us to set aside our own concerns and turn ourself toward the other person. But this basic openness may not be enough. By developing a range of behavioral skills, we enhance our capacity for empathy. An accepting posture, attentive listening, and sensitive paraphrasing contribute to our effective presense to other people.

Our posture gives another person important information about how important we judge them to be. If we appear distracted or edgy, if we keep glancing at our watch or if we rush to take an in-coming telephone call, the other person often feels slighted. If, on the other hand, we turn our chair toward our conversation partner, if we make eye contact and seem relaxed, we communicate that we want to be really present to them.

Learning to listen well is another important skill of community interaction. To listen is to pay attention; it is a receptive, not a passive, attitude. If we cannot pay attention, we do not hear; if we cannot listen, we do not understand and respond effectively. To listen well is to listen actively, alert to the full context of the message. The skills of active listening are those behaviors that enable us to be aware of another person's full message. This includes our being alert to another's words and nuance. But equally important are non-verbal factors. Another's tone of voice, gestures, and timing may tell us more than words. To listen actively, then, calls for an awareness of the content, the feelings, and the context of communication.

Sensitive paraphrasing is a skill of empathy as well. We show others that we understand by expressing the essence of their message. To paraphrase is not merely to "parrot," to repeat mechanically what has just been said. Rather, we want to show that we have really heard, that we appreciate not just the words but their significance. We go beyond a simple assurance that we understand by offering a statement of *what* we have understood. Our conversation partners can then confirm our understanding or clarify what we have misunderstood. In either case, we demonstrate our respect for other people and for what they have to say.

Empathy, then, is our ability to understand another's ideas, feelings, and values from within that person's world. Understanding is the goal of empathy; as such, it precedes evaluation. Empathy does not mean that we will always agree; it does not require that we accept another's point of view as our own or even as best for that person. We may have to evaluate the other person's ideas. We may have to negotiate as we move toward a decision we can share. But these movements of evalua-

tion and negotiation come later. Our first goal is to accurately understand the other person and the message. Judgment and decision are not
secondary in our communication, but they are subsequent to accurate
understanding.

This open stance of empathy does much to enhance communication
in collaborative work and communal life. But communication involves
more than receptivity. We must speak as well as listen, initiate as well
as understand. Personal disclosure thus becomes an essential skill of
community. To share our ideas or our concerns with others, we must
overcome the hesitancy suggested by fear or shame. But these inhibi-
tions overcome, we must share ourselves in ways fitting for us and for
our relationship. Appropriate self-disclosure can seem complicated.
But we are not limited to our current level of success. We can become
more skillful; we can learn better ways to express our values and needs,
our ideas and feelings.

Appropriate disclosure begins in self-awareness. We must *know*
what we have experienced, what we think, how we feel, what we need,
what we want to do. This knowledge will not be full and finished. In
fact, an unwillingness to speak until we are completely sure of ourself
can be a trap in communication. Self-awareness is the ability to know
where we are now, to be in touch with the dense and ambiguous information of our own life right now.

Beyond knowing our own insights and values, our needs and hopes,
we must *value* them. This need not mean that we are convinced they
are the best for everyone. Rather, we need to take our needs seriously
as deserving of examination and respect, both from ourselves and from
others. Our ideas and feelings, our perceptions of ourself and of the
world have worth and weight. By valuing them, we contribute to the
possibility that others can appreciate them as well. Assuredly, our
needs and purposes exist in a context of those of other people. But a
conviction that our insights and goals are valuable is basic to mature
self-disclosure.

An important skill of personal disclosure is our ability to speak concretely. We often thwart communication by using phrases like "Everyone knows..." (instead of "I think that..."), "Most people want..." (instead of "I need..."), or "People have a hard time..." (instead of "It's
difficult for me..."). For effective self-disclosure, we must learn to say
"I," to acknowledge our own ideas and concerns.

Beyond this willingness to own our experience, we can learn to provide more specific details about our actions and values and emotions. This challenge looks different in different settings. If we are to work effectively on a parish ministry team, for example, we must speak concretely to other people about what we are doing and about how we see our actions contributing to the common goal. Or, as lay persons becoming more aware of our baptismal call and ministry, we may need to expand our theological vocabulary so that we can describe our vision of the parish or our sense of personal vocation in ways that make sense to the larger church.

To share ourself with friends or in a support group, we will need a well-nuanced vocabulary of feelings, one that goes well beyond "I feel good" and "I feel bad." To tell someone that we feel good is to share some important information about ourself. But what does feeling good mean for us? Is this good feeling one of confidence? affection? physical health? Does the feeling result from something we have done or something that has been done for us? Is the person we are addressing an important part of this good feeling? Or, is this person incidental? In each of these instances, our self-disclosure becomes concrete when we name our emotional response more precisely and when we describe the events and actions that are part of these feelings.

Confrontation, too, makes a critical contribution to community. For most of us, the word "confrontation" implies conflict. But we use the word here with a meaning that goes beyond its narrow and, most often, negative connotation. The ability to confront involves the psychological strength to give (and receive) emotionally significant information in ways that lead to further exploration rather than to self-defense. Sometimes the emotionally significant information is more positive than negative. To say "I love you" is to share emotionally significant information. And many of us know that learning of another's love for us can be confrontive. Similarly, to give a compliment is to share emotionally significant information. And some of us defend ourselves against compliments as forcefully as other of us defend ourselves against accusations of blame! But confrontation is most often troublesome when the information we bring up is negative.

When we confront skillfully, this painful communication leads us to explore the difficulty rather than to defend ourselves against one another. Our ability to confront effectively is enhanced when we are able to speak descriptively rather than judgmentally. To tell a co-worker that we missed an important meeting because he took the staff car and brought it back late is to *describe,* but to call him selfish and inconsiderate is to *judge.* While both messages may be hard for our colleaque to hear, one is more likely to escalate into a quarrel than is the other. Judgment is not irrelevant in confrontation, but premature judgment short-circuits the process of exploration and mutual understanding. Perhaps extenuating circumstances caused him to be late; perhaps he is genuinely sorry that he inconvenienced us and wants to make amends. Our attack on his selfishness does not leave room for a positve response from him. Instead, he defends himself against our accusation, perhaps by calling up instances of our own selfishness, perhaps by leaving the scene altogether. In neither case has communication between us been furthered.

Other behaviors make our confrontation more effective, that is, more likely to further communication between us. These include the ability to accept feelings of anger in ourself and in others, and the ability to show respect even as we disagree. These skills become especially important in dealing with conflict in community settings.

Conflict and Community

Conflict is an aspect of Christian community about which our rhetoric can be misleading. In our ceremonies and sermons we often dwell upon images of unity and peace and joy. These images of life together as Christians are important and true, but partial. When, as a believing community, we refuse to speak about the more ambiguous experiences of anger and frustration and misunderstanding, we fail to tell the truth about our shared life.

Conflict and hostility are not goals of community. But neither are they automatic indications that our parish or ministry team or religious house is in serious trouble. As a normal and expected ingredient of any relationship (whether friendship or team work or family life), conflict draws people close and engages them at levels of their significant values and needs. Whenever we encounter each other over a period of time, especially when matters of importance are involved, we can anticipate that differences will be noted, disagreements will develop, discord may emerge. The challenge in community is not simply to do away with these signs of conflict or, worse, to refuse to admit them when they do arise. Rather, we can attempt to learn ways to recognize the potential areas of conflict *for us* and to deal with these issues and feelings in ways that strengthen rather than destroy the bonds between us.

Conflict, then, is a normal dynamic in relationships. We can expect to find it in communities because these groups are characterized by diversity as well as unity. The diversity that we find in community life can sometimes lead to an experience of discrepancy. And conflict usually arises in response to discrepancy. This discrepancy can be in interpretation (we each give different meaning to the same event), in expectation (things do not turn out as we expect; others do not act as we thought they had agreed), or in need (coming from different starting points, we look for different outcomes).

The presence of conflict between us can be an invitation to explore this discrepancy and thus to learn more about ourself and others. If we can discover the discrepancy to which our conflict points, we are in a better position to learn from it and to resolve the gap. But this opportunity for learning and for resolution is lost if we are unable to look into the conflict and if we turn instead to self-defense or to blame.

Conflict is more often a sign of a group's health than a symptom of disease. The presence of conflict most often indicates that we are about something that we feel is significant enough to generate the disturbances and tensions we are experiencing. Conflict marks a relationship of some force. Moreover, we can harness this energy; it need not work against us. Groups that have nothing important enough to fight about are more likely to die than are groups in which some dissension occurs. Indifference is a greater enemy of community than is conflict.

We can recognize conflict as a step toward the resolution of tension, as an impulse whose aim is reconciliation. But the power of conflict is ambiguous: it can lead not toward resolution but toward increased hostility, finally, to group disintegration. Many of us know and fear these painful results. Conflict feels bad. We feel angry or hurt; the other person feels rejected or resentful. Beyond these negative emotions, conflict leads to the deterioration of relationships. Sometimes the break comes immediately; sometimes we try to continue together, but a mounting burden of bitterness ultimately breaks the bonds between us. In the face of these memories of its distressing power, the realization that our communities may inevitably expect conflict alarms us.

But this dismal view does not reveal the full picture. Groups that do not anticipate conflict, that do not understand its potential contribution, are most likely to feel its negative effects. Groups that learn to face conflict, that develop explicit strategies to recognize and resolve discrepancies, are more likely to reap its benefits.

Facing Conflict

The experience of facing conflict together gives us greater confidence in a friendship; our relationship has been tested and has survived. Conflict, while remaining an ambiguous dynamic, can have this positive effect in a community's life as well. However, just as the presence of conflict does not necessarily signal a relationship in trouble, neither does it automatically result in new learning or deeper commitment. Whether conflict will have positive or negative effect is due in large part to how we respond. To deal with its ambiguous power, we must first appreciate that conflict's force *can* be more than just negative. We must believe that the benefits of working through our distress are worth the trouble and discomfort involved. We must develop the resources of personal maturity that enable us to face strong emotion, to look at ourselves anew, and to change. And we must display the skillful behaviors that help us deal effectively with one another even in the heat of our disagreement.

Resolving Conflict

Conflict's ambiguous power is put at the service of a group through expectation, recognition, and management. To harness its energy, we must *expect* that conflict will occur and that its presence can be positive. Anticipating we be able to manage conflict when it arises helps us sustain a positive approach. We can learn to *recognize* our own patterns of conflict, the issues or circumstances or exchanges by which it is evoked, the responses (avoidance, blame, control) our group tends to make. We can agree on more effective ways of dealing with discrepancy and opposition, holding ourselves and each other accountable to use these strategies to *manage* conflict when it does arise. The tools of conflict management are varied, ranging from the basic communication skills discussed earlier in this chapter to more comprehensive models of problem solving and negotiation. In the reference section at the end of this chapter, we list some useful guides to these skills and strategies of conflict resolution in groups.

For communities to flourish beyond the initial period of enthusiasm, we must develop among ourselves a sense of the appropriateness—or at least the inevitability—of conflict and a common understanding of how to deal with it. The methods we develop for conflict management do more than forestall problems. They can serve as channels through which our rich diversity is brought to awareness and put at the service of the community.

Conflict should not, of course, be the only or the chief dynamic among us. Communities must take care, especially during times of stress and dissension, to balance these with genuine expressions of solidarity and mutual concern. Often we achieve this most effectively in ritual and celebration.

This brings us back to the importance of skills for community interaction. Those of us who participate in communities, especially those of us who minister to communities, must nurture effective behavior in ourselves and others. We need communication skills: the ability to disclose information about ourselves, our needs and expectations, our images and definitions of community. To effectively incorporate diversity within our communities, we must develop skills of conflict resolution, negotiation, and problem solving. To enable us to dream beyond the discrepancies that divide us to a new solution where we can stand together, we need skills of empathy and imagination. We also need to celebrate well both our diversity and our unity. These tools—clarification, negotiation, imagination, and celebration—are clearly not all that is required for building up the community of faith. But without these tools, too often overlooked, the task becomes more burdensome.

FOR FURTHER REFLECTION

Recall your experience of communication and conflict in community life. Beginning in a mood of quiet, bring to mind the groups to which you belong. Spend time with this moment of recollection; let the memories come as they will, whether positive or negative, whether satisfying or unresolved.

From these several memories, choose one that is for you an instance of satisfying or successful communication in community. Let the example come to mind more fully and then consider: How was this experience satisfying for you? What did you bring to the experience? How did others contribute? What were your feelings during this exchange? How do you feel about it now?

Then turn to a memory of a difficult or unresolved exchange, perhaps a time of conflict. Can you identify the discrepancy at the root of this distress? In what ways did your behavior (and that of others) add to the tension? How did you (and others) try to resolve the problem? What were your feelings during this exchange? How do you feel about it now?

Finally, what learnings about communication and conflict do you take from this look at your own experience?

ADDITIONAL RESOURCES

Deborah Tannen provides clues for understanding the different communication styles of men and women in *You Just Don't Understand: Women and Men in Conversation* (New York: Ballantine, 1990). Gerard Egan continues his significant contribution to the theory and practice of skills training in a new edition of *The Skilled Helper* (Monterey, Cal.: Brooks/Cole, 1990). Robert Bolton examines the skills of effective communication in *People Skills: How to Assert Yourself, Listen to Others, and Resolve Conflict* (New York: Touchstone Books, 1986). In *The Skilled Participant: A Way to Effective Collaboration* (Notre Dame, Ind.: Ave Maria Press, 1988), Keith Clark develops a model of the personal skills needed to live and work effectively with others. Celia Allison Hahn probes the factors that complicate collaboration between women and men in *Sexual Paradox: Creative Tensions in Our Lives and in Our Congregations* (Pilgrim Press, 1991); see also Anne Marie Nuechterlein and Celia Allison Hahn, *The Male-Female Church Staff: Celebrating the Gifts, Confronting the Challenges* (Washington, D.C.: Alban Institute, 1990).

Speed Leas provides practical assistance for understanding and managing conflict in religious groups in *Discover Your Conflict Management Style* (Washington, D.C.: Alban Institute, 1985). Roger Fisher and William Ury have contributed significantly to the development of skills and strategies for dealing with conflict; see *Getting to Yes: Negotiating*

Agreement Without Giving In (New York: Penguin, 1981). See also Roger Fisher and Scott Brown, *Getting Together: Building a Relationship That Gets to Yes* (New York: Houghton Mifflin, 1988); William Ury, Jeanne M. Brett, and Stephen B. Goldberg, *Getting Disputes Resolved: Designing Systems to Cut the Costs of Conflict* (San Francisco: Jossey-Bass, 1990); and William Ury, *Getting Past No: Negotiating with Difficult People* (New York: Bantam, 1991).

In *Putting Forgiveness Into Practice* (Nashville: Abingdon Press, 1986), Doris Donnelly gives graceful insight into the tasks of personal and communal reconciliation; see also her "Binding Up Wounds in a Healing Community," in Michael J. Henchal, ed. *Repentance and Reconciliation in the Church* (Collegeville, Minn.: Liturgical Press, 1987). Dominique Barbe defines a theology of nonviolent action in *A Theology of Conflict* (Maryknoll, N.Y.: Orbis Books, 1989). *In Managing Church Conflict* (Philadelphia: Westminster, 1991), Hugh Halverstadt provides practical ground rules for dealing effectively with conflict in religious groups.

CHAPTER FIFTEEN

COMMUNITY IN THE LIFE OF THE MINISTER

The communal dimensions of ministry receive new emphasis today. Theology and pastoral practice alike stress the corporate reality of the Christian mission. As a result, three kinds of social groupings are familiar to many persons in ministry. We can identify these groupings as support network, faith community, and ministry team. Sometimes these three terms are used as synonyms, as though each referred to the same kind of group, the same quality of interpersonal experience. But experience and analysis, however, suggest this is not the case.

Faith community, support network, and ministry team designate three quite distinct social relationships. Each has its own particular objectives, its own dynamics, its own pressures and rewards. Each contributes to the vitality of the Christian minister. But the three are not equivalent concepts. And, most often, they are not the same in our experience. The identical group of persons *can* serve one another as a principal source of personal support, as a visible community of shared values, and as colleagues in collaborative action. But functioning in these multiple roles for one another is never easy.

We can make an initial distinction among these three relationships in terms of their different orientations. A support network focuses on "I," the self. A community focuses on "we," the visible grouping of persons. And a ministry team focuses on "task," the job to be done. Distinguishing this way is, obviously, too simple. However, it is the first step in clarifying these different forms of social experience.

Personal Support Network

Our personal support network is made up of those persons whose presence, support, and challenge enable our personal and professional life to flourish. We speak of a "support network" rather than a "support group." A group generally refers to persons all of whom are in relation to one another. We may belong to a "support group" like this, several people who know each other and interact together on a regular basis for mutual encouragement and growth. But the sources of support for our personal and professional life will extend beyond such a recognizable group, to include people who have a particular relationship with us but who are not part of a group with one another. Many of us, for example, have looked forward to introducing to each other two persons who are each important to us, only to find that these two have no real basis for friendship between themselves. In this instance, both the friends may be part of our own support network, though the three of us do not, precisely speaking, constitute a "group."

Our close friends stand at the heart of our support network; some members of our family, as well, are likely to share this priority of place. But the network will also include persons whose relationship with us does not have the mutuality of friendship or close family ties. For example, we may develop an ongoing relationship with a spiritual director, a person who assists our efforts to discern and respond to the movements of God in our life. This relationship may be critical to our development as a person of faith and as a minister, yet our companion here need not be a close personal friend.

Colleagues in ministry and other professional peers are often sources of information, encouragement, and critique; these people nurture our professional life by supporting our development as competent ministers. At particular points in our career, we may seek regular contact with a ministry supervisor, as part of a commitment to improve our professional effectiveness. At other times, we may benefit from regular discussions with a physician or a psychological counselor. These are the kinds of relationships that build up a personal support network.

There are two senses in which "I" is the focus of a network of personal support. First, and most obviously, our own needs give shape to the network. This statement can be disconcerting because it appears to contradict the call to selfless service that should characterize ministry. But increasingly, we realize that personal development is neither irrelevant to nor distracting from our life with God. As the long experience of the church shows us, the quality of ministry depends in large part on the quality of those who minister. And most of us sense, even more immediately, that our own effectiveness in ministry is directly related to the level of our spiritual, intellectual, and emotional development. Developing a support network helps us stay accountable in each of these areas.

This brings us to the second sense in which "I" is the focus of a personal support network. Passively waiting for circumstances to provide us with the kinds of friends or colleagues we need is risky. As adult Christians, we are responsible for developing those relationships that challenge us beyond mediocrity and support our continuing development as faithful and vital ministers. The discipline required to initiate and maintain these supportive relationships is part of the contemporary asceticism of our vocation.

Faith Community

Many of us in ministry desire to be part of a visible "we," an identifiable group with whom we can share the significant values and important purposes of our life. The "we" of community can be visible in a variety of ways: through common residence (such as a convent or rectory or commune); through shared membership (such as a faith sharing group or intentional community or ministry staff); or through the activities of a more loosely defined movement (such as the women's movement or the ecological movement or the peace movement).

But faith communities go further. Whatever the predominant source of our group's visibility—whether joint activities or common membership or shared residence—most of us expect our life together to include more. We express this expanded hope in our desire that faith sharing and mutual support be part of our community experience.

Both faith sharing and mutual support are challenging in the church today. In this time of profound transition and institutional purification, we expectably find differences among us regarding acceptable styles of shared prayer and preferred forms of communal worship. A community with flexibility and tolerance discovers that this diversity is enriching. But in many church settings these days, controversy over religious expression makes faith sharing difficult. Instead of opening our hearts to one another, we feel the need to defend ourselves. This defensive stance defeats a community's hope to be a place where the fragile story of our own lives of faith can be shared and celebrated. Developing appropriate forms of communal prayer demands sensitivity to our diversity and to the recent and sometimes painful history of change in the church. But if our communities are to thrive, we must make this effort.

In our communities today we also expect a shared experience of genuine support. This does not mean that only close friends can form communities. As we have noted frequently, friendship and community are not synonyms. But neither are they antonyms. Communities are strengthened in many ways when members like each other. But personal friendship is only one of the values around which communities may form. For many of us, a common ministry commitment—whether to economic justice, to institutional reform, to quality education for the poor, or to affirming to religious significance of suffering—can sustain us in community with persons who share those values but who are not our close personal friends. As members of communities like this—with a strong task focus—we must take special care to insure that the task is not the only bond among us. Without opportunities for personal exchange and mutual support, our sense of community will disintegrate. Fortunately, mutual support can find many expressions. As our range of interpersonal experience broadens, we become aware of the various ways in which we show our care for one another. Drawing on this awareness, faith communities can develop satisfying styles for giving and receiving the gift of genuine concern.

Team Ministry

Increasingly today, the tasks of ministry draw people toward greater collaboration. In the logic of team ministry, we come together to accomplish corporately a task that we could not achieve, or could not achieve as well, alone. A ministry group functioning as a team makes decisions in light of some basic questions: Does this facilitate the task? Does this promote our ministry?

Since the circumstances of most ministry teams are complex, the response to these questions can be somewhat complicated. We see the complexity first in the range of motives that influence the decision to join the team. Many of us seek out a team in the conviction that joint action can accomplish what our individual effort cannot: "In this group, we will accomplish more than any of us can alone." Coordinated planning and collaborative action characterize ministry teams that share this conviction.

Other teams develop with the explicit goal of providing mutual support and encouragement among those involved in work that is particularly challenging. In these instances, coordinated planning and joint action may be secondary to the more pervasive goal of sustaining one another in the midst of difficult or frustrating tasks. Clusters formed among inner-city parishes and alliances established among people in justice ministries are often teams in this sense.

For some of us, the theological conviction that Christian ministry is always a communal activity, that it can never be done "alone," guides our move toward team ministry. Convinced that the witness provided by the ongoing effort to work together in honesty and respect stands at the core of the good news that Christians have to share with women and men today, we see community as an integral part of the "task" of a ministry team.

Any one person's choice for team ministry is likely to be influenced by a combination of reasons. The job that is available, our previous experience in both autonomous and cooperative ministry, and a sense of both personal strengths and limitations influence the decision. Multiple motives are the rule rather than the exception. This complexity introduces complications into the team's functioning. Achieving simultaneously several different goals of team membership is difficult. The demands of the shared task may dominate, crowding out the time we need for mutual support and critique. A commitment to proceed by consensus decision making may delay effective action. Actions we take to achieve one goal in the team's life may undermine another. A program of performance evaluation may contribute to the success of a ministry project and yet foster a destructive sense of competition among us. Time spent in personal sharing will strengthen our sense of cohesion but risks diverting energy away from the pressing demands of our work. A ministry team that intends several goals—effective collaboration, mutual support, communal witness—must be aware that each has its own set of requirements, each makes its own particular demands. While these complications do not signal that team ministry is impossible, they remind us how ambitious a hope it is.

The same group of people *can* function for each other as support group, faith community, and ministry team. But while that is possible, it is seldom easy. Each of these ways to be together makes its own special demands. And sometimes we can experience these differing demands as contradictory. Our commitment to support a colleague through a difficult time in his personal life may conflict with our commitment to meet a critical deadline in our shared ministry. A group assumes many responsibilities when its members choose to be for one another a visible community, a support network, and a ministry team. This situation offers clear advantages but inherent strains exist as well. We must anticipate that such a group will experience, from time to time, the antagonisms inherent in its members' multiple responsibilities to one another. Many religious groups are unprepared for this. They interpret these strains as an indication of group weakness or individual selfishness, not as a normal and expected part of such a complex undertaking.

If our group has not come to an explicit awareness of the range of goals and motives among us, the situation becomes even more difficult. As members, we may have differing images of what our group is about, differing expectations of how we deal with one another. We must expect this diversity, especially in the early stages of our group's life. But tensions are likely to increase among us if we do not recognize and resolve these contrasting images and expectations.

Clarification is a starting point in the effort to understand our life together in groups. Compromise, the effort to reach a satisfactory resolution of our differences, is a continuing dynamic in groups that survive and thrive. Compromise has as central a role in friendship as it does in planning and problem solving. The dual process of clarification and compromise will be indispensable for any group attempting to discern its various obligations and to mediate among the legitimate demands to which these give rise. Christian ministry is a corporate undertaking. An awareness of the diversity of group forms and a respect for the power and limit of each will contribute to the vitality of the ministry and the creativity of the minister.

FOR FURTHER REFLECTION

Consider these three social groupings in your own life.

1. Who are the persons who make up your own network of personal support?

2. Where do you participate in "a visible grouping of shared value and purpose"? Who is with you in this community?

3. Are you part of a team in ministry? Who are the members of this work group?

4. Chart the areas of overlap, noting the persons who are part of more than one of these groupings. What are the positive effects of this overlap, the ways in which your relationship or your work is enhanced?

5. Are there any negative effects of this overlap, ways in which your relationship or work is complicated?

ADDITIONAL RESOURCES

Mary E. Hunt explores the theological significance of friendship in *Fierce Tenderness: A Feminist Theology of Friendship* (New York: Crossroad, 1990). Lillian Rubin's compelling analysis of the role of friendship in the lives of American women and men is found in *Just Friends* (New York: HarperCollins, 1985). Stuart Miller focuses on men's experience in *Men and Friendship* (Boston: Houghton Mifflin, 1983); Janice Raymond examines women's experience in *A Passion for Friends* (Boston: Beacon Press, 1986).

Roy M. Oswald offer practical help in developing a network of personal support in *How to Build a Support System for Your Ministry* (Washington, D.C.: Alban Institute, 1991). Rose Marie Jasinski and Peter Foley describe efforts by congregations of vowed religious to encourage wider communal involvement in "The Associate Movement in Religious Life," *Review for Religious* (May-June, 1990), pp. 353-357. In *Poets, Prophets and Pragmatists: Challenges of Pluralism to Religious Life* (Notre Dame, Ind.: Ave Maria Press, 1988), Evelyn M. Woodward offers a theological analysis of community life that is well suited to many forms of intentional faith community. Barbara Fiand records the rich heritage of varied community living in *Where Two or Three are Gathered: Community Life for the Contemporary Religious* (New York: Crossroad, 1992).

Loughlan Sofield and Carrol Juliano provide practical tools for strengthening community among people working together in *Collaborative Ministry* (Notre Dame, Ind.: Ave Maria Press, 1987).

Of Related Interest

GOOD THINGS HAPPEN
Experiencing Community in Small Groups
Dick Westley

Dick Westley explores the mysterious and
sacred nature of community. He shows how,
despite its significance in the divine order,
community often makes its appearance amid
the mundane flow of everyday life. For
those who hunger for a meaningful small
faith community experience, this book offers
an understanding of experience, as well as
practical suggestions and guidelines for both
beginning groups and those already
established.
ISBN: 0-89622-512-7, 5 1/2" X 8 1/2",
Paper,160 pages, $9.95

FORMING A SMALL CHRISTIAN COMMUNITY
A Personal Journey
Richard Currier and Frances Gram

Readers are provided historical and
theological foundations for forming a small
Christian community, and are also offered
practical step-by-step guidance for going
through the process. Each of the seven
chapters contains a series of questions and
answers that address the concerns of
community members, as well as discussion
questions for group use.
ISBN: 0-89622-511-9, 5 1/2" X 8 1/2",
Paper,178 pages, $7.95

Available at religious bookstores or from
TWENTY-THIRD PUBLICATIONS
P.O. Box 180 • Mystic, CT 06355
1-800-321-0411